"An adventure story, a prose hymn to her native land, and a morality tale for the whole world."

—Joseph Barnes, *New York Herald Tribune*

"Here . . . is the philosophy of the meaning of betrayal, the basic tenets of loyalty, the factors in society and humanity that gave birth to the forms of treason represented by such figures as William Joyce (better known as Lord Haw-Haw) . . . The quality of the British fascists, the Mosely followers—the steps of Nazi penetration and the use they put their tools, the degradation in the office of propaganda—the forming of the British Free Corps to fight their fellow Britishers, a corps drawn from the prisoner of war camps—the mental unbalance, rooted in childhood insecurities, of many of the traitors—the scorn in which some of them were held by the Germans. Here are some of the instruments by which nations are enslaved—'traitors incidentally, gangsters essentially.' The courtroom scenes are unforgettable . . . but the permanent value of the book lies in the study of the factors behind the various forms treason took; and in the brilliance of the style. A book for the long haul."

—*Kirkus Reviews*

"A meticulously accurate account of some of the most astounding and disturbing events in this disturbed age. It is a penetrating analysis of the men and the means by which these events were brought about. It is a detailed impeachment . . . a scathing indictment . . . a model of brilliant and effective writing."

—Struthers Burt, *Saturday Review*

"The great value of [West's] book is that it places before us one of the most significant problems of our times . . . with a searching and humane perception, and compels the reader's attention throughout by a brilliant use of word and phrase and image. It is an exciting, fascinating, and sometimes painful book."

—*Time and Tide*

"Rebecca West was one of the giants and will have a lasting place in English literature. No one in this century wrote more dazzling prose, or had more wit, or looked at the intricacies of human character and the ways of the world more intelligently."

—William Shawn

RADIO TREASON

RADIO TREASON

THE TRIALS OF LORD HAW-HAW, THE BRITISH VOICE OF NAZI GERMANY

REBECCA WEST

WITH A FOREWORD BY KATIE ROIPHE

McNally Editions

New York

McNally Editions
134 Prince St.
New York, NY 10012

ISBN: 978-1-94602-280-6
E-book: 978-1-94602-281-3

Design by Jonathan Lippincott

1   3   5   7   9   10   8   6   4   2

CONTENTS

Foreword by Katie Roiphe • ix

Chapter 1 • 3

Chapter 2 • 30

Chapter 3 • 53

Chapter 4 • 59

Chapter 5 • 84

Chapter 6 • 104

Chapter 7 • 130

Chapter 8 • 153

Chapter 9 • 170

FOREWORD

In December 1947, fifty-five-year-old Rebecca West, holding a cup of tea, appeared on the cover of *Time* magazine, which declared her "indisputably the world's No. 1 woman writer." But in the decades that followed she has fallen out of fashion, her sparkling, wholly original essays no longer read and celebrated by the broader public. Since her death in 1983, West's great, spirited work has been lost to all but the most dedicated readers. This is a huge shame. As William Shawn, then the editor in chief of the *New Yorker* put it, "No one in this century wrote more dazzling prose, or had more wit, or looked at the intricacies of human character and the ways of the world more intelligently."

Born Cicily Isabel Fairfield, she took the nom de plume Rebecca West and rose to prominence at the age of nineteen by writing fiery pieces in the suffragette magazines *The Freewoman* and *The New Freewoman* and in the socialist newspaper *The Clarion*. Her feminism, though, was always that of a passionately independent thinker. She once made fun of one of the suffragists from *The New Freewoman* "who was always jumping up and asking us to be kind to illegitimate children, as if we all made a habit of seeking out illegitimate children and insulting them!"

In her witty, eviscerating reviews, West took on several of the great male writers of the day. She became known for these eviscerations. As George Bernard Shaw put it, "Rebecca West could handle a pen as brilliantly as ever I could and much more savagely." Men weren't the only ones who viewed her as impressive and slightly alarming. Virginia Woolf wrote, "Rebecca is a cross between a charwoman and gypsy, but as tenacious as a terrier, with flashing eyes, very shabby, rather dirty nails, immense vitality, bad taste, suspicion of intellectuals and great intelligence."

Indeed, she was a vivid presence on the page and off. At twenty-one, she had an affair with H. G. Wells and bore his child in secret. Over the arc of her long career, she wrote novels as well as essays, reviews, and literary reporting. She was particularly drawn to the human drama of trials, her reporting ranging from a London murder trial, in "Mr. Setty and Mr. Hume," to a lynching trial in South Carolina, to the Nuremberg trials; she liked a dramatic public event that allowed her to theorize social relations, observe characters, and give what today we might call close readings of the culture.

In 1945, the *New Yorker* commissioned West to write a series of dispatches from the London trial of William Joyce, who stood accused of collaborating with the Nazis. The trial ended on a Thursday, and to the amazement of her editors, West cabled in the first installment of her remarkable series the very next day. In *Radio Treason*, she tells the story of a schoolteacher, and English fascist, who went to Nazi

Germany and became a radio personality, broadcasting
Nazi propaganda during the war.

Without ever hiding her disdain for Joyce (a "puny,
undistinguished little man who was wild with a desire
for glory"; "He looked like an ugly Scott Fitzgerald, but
more nervous"), West used him as a case study, delving
deep into the psychology of a gifted talker rejected and
slighted by the higher echelons of British society. In the
process, she identifies a recurring type on the far right:
"the white-collar man who cannot climb up because he
has no special talent to make his own ladder and society
will not let him use its existing ladders, which are reserved
for other people." She identifies a simmering rage of exclusion, a consciousness of snobbism, of a destiny always just
outside the inner circles of success, which animates the
turn toward fascism.

One of the joys of reading Rebecca West is the
near-sensual pleasure of her sentences. She tells us, "The
gray stone of the Old Bailey had been gashed by a bomb.
Its solidity had been sliced as if it were a cake, and the
walls of the slice were a crude new brick." She describes
a Nazi testifying in a trial as "a lank and hollow-cheeked
young man, who might have been carved in wood in the
thirteenth century." She describes another traitor whose
"character was like an automobile that will not hold the
road."

West is the natural predecessor of brilliant stylists
Janet Malcolm and Joan Didion, who may very well have
curled up reading her *New Yorker* essays in their teens. Like
Malcolm, West performed a rigorous psychological analysis
of her subjects. The critic V. S. Pritchett talks about West

milking "the accidental gesture, the unguarded remark, until it yields its comment on human corruption."

Like Didion, West was also a master at mood painting. One detects traces of West's trial narratives in Didion's great piece of crime writing "Sentimental Journeys," which interrogates the spectacle of the Central Park jogger rape case in 1990. In that piece, Didion describes a reporter's view of criminal cases as "windows on the city or culture in which they take place, opportunities to enter not only households but parts of the culture normally closed." This could be a description of West's modus operandi in the courtroom.

Long before the dawn of the New Journalism in the '60s, Rebecca West brought the brio of fiction to her factual writing. Her innovative reporting fused psychological speculation, personal reactions, and cultural readings into elegant and ambitious meditations. She was also a master of plot and suspense. Although Truman Capote's *In Cold Blood* (1966) is often described as the first "nonfiction novel," Capote credited West, in a *Paris Review* interview, as a pioneer of the form. She used her reporting to shade characters and create rich imaginative narratives of her subject's inner thoughts and motivations; she crafted novellas out of real life. In *Radio Treason*, she glides into Joyce's consciousness, takes the time to linger on his motivations and grievances to lovingly evoke a character, while also coolly condemning him as a traitor. She writes, "That he deserved pity was noted by the intellect; pity was not felt."

West also captures the mood of the public watching the spectacle, the wrung-out exhaustion of postwar

England, the hardness of those who had kept calm and carried on. She writes that Joyce's evident bravery in the face of his death sentence might have moved them in another time.

> But every man and every woman who attended Joyce's trial had at some time during the last six years been in danger of undeserved death or pain, and had shown, or seen others showing great courage. William Joyce could not make any claim on them by being pitiful or brave. He could not arouse their interest because it was exceptional to meet violent death, since he was in the dock by reason of failure to acquit himself well when that had been their common destiny. So they turned away from him and left the court as if it had been a cinema or concert.

Her exquisite linguistic precision opens doors to a deeper understanding of the cultural moment. Large political abstractions become crystal clear in a single turn of phrase. Take her description of fascism as "drunkenness without laughter." Whole unsettling chapters of history snap into focus with that phrase.

The last time I read Rebecca West's account of the treason trial was ten years ago and it felt safely historical. Reading it now, it is impossible to avoid the contemporary resonances. It is as if Lord Haw-Haw has been transported from her time into ours. We have our own rejected, looked-down-upon young men who are delivered by political extremism into a feeling of acceptance. Our own Lord Haw-Haws gather in sub-Reddits and TikTok and Telegram. They revel in Trump rallies and Truth Social and Newsmax.

One thinks, watching the rise of Trumpism, of the great insult William Joyce carried within him. One thinks of the rage sparked by Hillary Clinton's peculiar, offhand condemnation of the "basket of deplorables." One thinks of the motley crowd breaking into the Capitol when one reads West's lines about Lord Haw-Haw: "What else could he have ever done but use his trick of gathering other poor fellows luckless in the same way, so that they might overturn the sane community that was bound to reject them, and substitute a mad one that would regard them kindly?"

Katie Roiphe
New York, 2025

RADIO TREASON

CHAPTER 1

The idea of a traitor first became real to the British of our time when they heard the voice of William Joyce on the radio during the war. The conception of treachery first became real to them when he was brought to trial as a radio traitor. For he was something new in the history of the world. Never before have people known the voice of one they had never seen as well as if he had been a husband or a brother or a close friend; and had they foreseen such a miracle they could not have imagined that this familiar unknown would speak to them only to prophesy their death and ruin. A great many people had experienced that hideous novelty, for it was easy to chance on Joyce's wave-length when one was tuning-in on the English stations, and there was a rasping yet rich quality about his voice which made it difficult not to go on listening, and he was nearly convincing in his assurance. It seemed as if one had better hearken and take warning when he suggested that the destiny of the people he had left in England was death, and the destiny of his new masters in Germany life and conquest, and that, therefore, his listeners had better change sides and submit; and he had the advantage that the news in the papers confirmed what he said. He was not only alarming, he was ugly. He opened a vista into a mean life. He always spoke as if he were better fed and better clothed than we were, and so, we now know, he was. He went farther than that mockery of his own people's plight. He sinned that sin which travesties legitimate hatred because it is felt for kindred, as incest is the travesty of legitimate love. When the U-boats were sinking so many of our ships that to open the newspapers was to see the faces of drowned sailors, he rolled the figures of our lost tonnage on his tongue. When we were facing the hazard of D-day, he rejoiced in the thought of the English dead which would soon lie under the West Wall.

So all the curious went off to the Central Criminal Court on 17 September 1945 when he came up for trial. The Old Bailey was as it had not been before the war and is not now. Because of the blitz it stood in a beautiful desert of charred stone. Churches stood blackened but apparently intact; birds, however, flew through the empty sockets of the windows and long grass grew around their altars. A red-brick Georgian mansion, hidden for a century by sordid warehouses, looked at the dome of St Paul's, now astonishingly great, across acres where willow-herb, its last purple flowers passing into silver clouds of seed dust, and yellow ragwort grew from the ground plan of a city drawn in rubble. The grey stone of the Old Bailey itself had been gashed by a bomb. Its solidity had been sliced as if it were a cake, and the walls of the slice were crude new red brick. Inside the building, because there was not yet the labour to take down the heavy blackout, the halls and passages and stairs were in perpetual dusk. The court-room—Court No. 1 where all the most famous criminal trials of modern times have taken place—was lit by electric light, for the shattered glass dome had not yet been rebuilt. Bare boards filled it in, giving an odd-come-short look to what had been a fine room in its austere way.

The strong light was merciless to William Joyce, whose appearance was a shock to all of us who knew him only over the air. His voice had suggested a large and flashy handsomeness, but he was a tiny little creature and not handsome at all. His hair was mouse-coloured and sparse, particularly above his ears, and his pinched and misshapen nose was joined to his face at an odd angle. His eyes were hard and shiny, and above them his thick eyebrows were pale and irregular. His neck was long, his shoulders narrow and sloping, his arms very short and thick. His body looked flimsy and coarse. There was nothing individual about him except a deep scar running across his right cheek from his ear to the corner of his mouth. But this did not create the savage and marred distinction that it might suggest, for it gave a mincing immobility to his small mouth. He was dressed with a dandyish preciosity, which gave no impression of well-being, only of nervousness. He was like an ugly version of Scott Fitzgerald, but more nervous. He moved with a jerky formality, and when he bowed to the judge his bow seemed sincerely respectful but entirely inappropriate to the occasion, and it was difficult to think of any occasion to which it would have been appropriate.

He had been defying us all. Yet there was nobody in the court who did not look superior to him. The men and women in the jury-box were all middle-aged, since the armies had not yet come home, and like everybody else in England at that date, they were puffy and haggard. But they were all the more pleasant to look at and more obviously trustworthy than the homely and eccentric little man in the dock; and compared with the judicial bench which he faced he was, of course, at an immense disadvantage, as we all should be, for its dignity is authentic. The judge sat in a high-backed chair, the sword of justice in its jewelled scabbard affixed to the oak panel behind him, splendid in his scarlet robe with its neckband of fine white linen and its deep cuffs and sash of purplish-black taffeta. Beside him, their chairs set farther back as a sign of their inferiority to him, sat the Lord Mayor of London and two aldermen, wearing antique robes of black silk with flowing white cravats and gold chains with pendant badges of office worked in precious metals and enamel. It sometimes happens, and it happened then, that these pompous trappings are given real significance by the faces of men who wear them. Judges are chosen for intellect and character, and city magnates must have risen through shrewdness combined with competence, at the least, and both must have the patience to carry out tedious routines over decades, and the story is often written on their features.

Looking from the bench to the dock, it could be seen that not in any sane community would William Joyce have had the ghost of a chance of holding such offices as these. This was tragic, as appeared when he was asked to plead and he said, 'Not guilty'. Those two words were the most impressive uttered during the trial. The famous voice was let loose. For a fraction of a second we heard its familiar quality. It was as it had sounded for six years, reverberating with the desire for power. Never was there a more perfect voice for a demagogue, for its reverberations were certain to awake echoes in every heart tumid with the same desire. Given this passionate ambition to exercise authority, which as this scene showed could not be gratified, what could he ever have done but use his trick of gathering together other poor fellows luckless in the same way, so that they might overturn the sane community that was bound to reject them and substitute a mad one that would regard them kindly?

That was the reason why he was in the dock; that, and Irish history. For it was at once apparent that this trial, like the great treason trial of the First World War which sent Sir Roger Casement to the gallows, had started on the other side of the St George's Channel. There had been rumours that Joyce was Irish, but they had never been officially confirmed, and his account was difficult to identify. But there was no doubt about it when one saw him in the dock. He had the real Donnybrook air. He was a not very fortunate example of the small, nippy, jig-dancing kind of Irish peasant, and the appearance of his brother, who attended the court every day in a state of great suffering, proved the family's origin. Quentin Joyce, who was then twenty-eight, was eleven years William's junior. He was the better-looking of the two with a sturdy body, a fresh colour, thick, lustrous brown hair, and the soft eyes of a cow. Nobody could mistake him for anything but a country-bred Irishman, and there were as clear traces of Irish origin in many of the followers of Joyce who watched the trial. True, his best friend was visibly a Scot; a black Highlander, with fierce black eyes blazing behind thick glasses, a tiny fuzz of black hair fancifully arranged on his prematurely bald head, and wrists and ankles as thin as lead piping. He was Angus MacNab, the former editor of a Fascist paper. He was plainly foredoomed to follow odd by-paths, and a variation in circumstances might have found him just as happily a spiritualist medium or a believer in the lost ten tribes of Israel. As it was, he was wholly committed to Joyce. So too were the rank and file of the faithful, who were for the most part men of violent and unhappy appearance, with a look of animal shyness and ferocity, and in some cases a measure of animal beauty. They were on the whole rather darker than one would expect in subscribers to the Aryan theory. One, especially, looked like a true gipsy. Many of them had an Irish cast of feature, and some bore Irish names. It was to be remembered that Joyce had seceded from Mosley's movement some years before the war and had started his own. These were not at all like Mosleyites, who were as a rule of a more varied and more cheerfully brutal type.

The case was tinged with irony from the start because the prosecuting counsel for the Crown was Sir Hartley Shawcross, the Attorney-General appointed by the new Labour Government. People in court were anxious to see what he was like, for when the Labour party had previously held office they had experienced some difficulty in getting Law Officers of the quality the Tories could provide; and it was a relief to find that he was a winning personality with a gift for setting out a lucid argument in the manner of a great advocate. He was, in fact, certain to enjoy just that worldly success which the man he was prosecuting had desired so much as to put himself in danger of a capital charge; a capital charge of which he was sure, it seemed in the earlier parts of the case, to be convicted.

There were three counts in the indictment brought against him. He had offended, it seemed, against the root of the law against treason; a Statute in which Edward III, in the year 1351, 'at the request of the lords and commons' declared that 'if a man do levy war against our Lord the King in his realm or be adherent to the King's enemies in his realm, giving them aid and comfort in the realm or elsewhere', he was guilty of treason. So the Clerk of the Court, Sir Wilfred Knops, said: 'William Joyce, you are charged in an indictment containing three counts with high treason. The particulars in the first count are that on the 18th September 1939 and on other days between that day and the 29th May 1945, you, being a person owing allegiance to our lord the King, and when a war was being carried on by the German realm against our King, did traitorously adhere to the King's enemies, in parts beyond the seas, that is to say in Germany, by broadcasting propaganda. In a second count of the same indictment, it is charged that you, on the 26th September 1940, being a person owing allegiance as in the other count, adhered to the King's enemies by purporting to become naturalized as a subject of Germany. And in the third count, the particulars are the same as in the first count, that is to say, you are charged with broadcasting propaganda, but the dates are different, and the dates in this case are the 18th September 1939, and on days between that day and the 2nd July 1940.' Later the first two counts were amended, for reasons emerging during the trial, and he was described in them as 'a British subject', but, significantly, no such change was made in the third.

It seemed as if William Joyce must be found guilty on the first two of these counts. What was first told of his life in court showed it as an open and shut case. William Joyce's dead father had been a Galway man named Michael Joyce, who had worked as a builder and contractor in America during the nineties. He married in May 1902 a Lancashire girl named Gertrude Emily Brooke in New York at the Roman Catholic Church of All Saints on Madison Avenue and 129th, and had settled down with her in Brooklyn where William had been born in 1906. Later inquiry into the story behind the evidence showed their life to have been very pleasant. The Joyces must have been quite prosperous. They lived in a very agreeable house, now an estate agent's office, on a corner lot in a broad street planted with trees, charming with the square, substantial, moderate charm of old Brooklyn. Now that street is occupied at one end by Negroes and at the other by Italians, but then it was a centre of the staider Irish, and the solid *bourgeois* German quarter was not far off.

In 1909 he took his family back to Ireland: a decision he must often have regretted. But at the time it must still have been very happy. By the time the First World War broke out he was the owner of considerable house property in County Mayo and County Galway, and he was manager of the horse-tramway system in Galway.

In 1922 he left Ireland, because it had become Eire. He was one of those native Irish who were against their own kind, and on the side of the English oppressor. Nowadays we recognize the existence of such people, but fancy them quislings, which is quite often unjust. Doubtless some of them were seduced by bribery dispensed by Dublin Castle, but many, and among those we must include Michael Joyce, were people who honestly loved law and order and preferred the smart uniforms and soldierly bearing of the English garrisons and the Royal Irish Constabulary to the furtive slouching of a peasantry distracted by poverty and revolutionary fever. The error of such people was insufficient inquiry into first causes, but for simple natures who went by surface indications the choice was natural enough.

In any case Michael Joyce paid the price of his convictions, and it was not light. He came to England for three very good reasons. The first was that the horse-tramways in Galway were abolished. One may deduce that he was a man of courage because he apparently ranked that reason as equal in importance to the other two, which were that his neighbours had been so revolted by his British sympathies that they burned down his house, and that he had been confused in many people's mind with an informer, also called Michael Joyce, who had denounced a priest to the Black and Tans. (It must be noted that William Joyce's father was indeed innocent of this crime, and, so far as is known, of any other; the identity of the other Michael Joyce was well established.)

On arriving in England the Joyces settled in Lancashire, and William alone made his way down to London, where he enrolled as a science student at Battersea Polytechnic. In August 1922 he, being sixteen years of age, sent a letter of application to the London University Officers' Training Corps, in which he said he wanted to study with a view to being nominated by the University for a commission in the

Regular Army. This letter was read in court, and it is very touching. It must have startled the recipient. It would not (nor would the note Joyce's father wrote later in support of the application) have convinced him that by the still snobbish standards of 1922 this was a likely candidate for the officers' mess, but it had another point of interest. 'I have served with the irregular forces of the Crown in an Intelligence capacity, against the Irish guerrillas. In command of a squad of sub-agents I was subordinate to the late Captain P. W. Keating, 2nd R.U.R., who was drowned in the *Egypt* accident. I have a knowledge of the rudiments of Musketry, Bayonet Fighting, and Squad Drill.' The *Egypt* was sunk off Ushant in May 1922; which meant that if this story were true the boy was engaged in guerrilla fighting with the Black and Tans when he was fifteen years old. The story was true. A photograph of him taken at that time shows him in a battledress, and a number of people remembered this phase of his life. Later, on an official form, he gave the duration of his service as four months, and named the regiment with which he had been associated as the Worcestershires. Further confirmation was given during his trial by an old man from County Galway who stood in the crowd outside and expressed to bystanders his hearty desire that William Joyce should be hanged for treason against the King of England, on the ground that he had worked with the Black and Tans in persecuting the Irish when they were revolting against the English. The crowd, with that toleration which foreigners possibly correctly suspect of being a form of smugness, was amused by the inconsistency.

But there was something in the letter more relevant to his trial.

•

I must now [wrote Joyce] mention a point which I hope will not give rise to difficulties. I was born in America, but of British parents. I left America when two years of age, have not returned since, and do not propose to return. I was informed, at the brigade headquarters of the district in which I was stationed in Ireland, that I possessed the same rights and privileges as I would if of natural British birth. I can obtain testimonials as to my loyalty to the Crown. I am in no way connected with the United States of America, against which, as against all other nations, I am prepared to draw the sword in British interests. As a young man of pure British descent, some of whose forefathers have held high position in the British army, I have always been desirous of devoting what little capability and energy I may possess to the country which I love so dearly. I ask that you may inform me if the accident of my birth, to which I refer above, will affect my position. I shall be in London for the September Matriculation Examination and I hope to commence studies at the London University at the beginning of the next academic year. I trust that you will reply as soon as possible, and that your reply will be favourable to my aspirations.

At an interview with an official of the O.T.C. he conveyed that he was 'in doubt as to whether he was a "British subject of pure European descent",' a doubt which must have been honest if he expressed it at all in view of the ardent hope expressed in his letter; but he asserted that his father had never been naturalized. This the father confirmed when the official wrote to him for further particulars.

> Dear Sir, your letter of the 23rd October received. Would have replied sooner, but have been away from home. With regard to my son William. He was born in America, I was born in Ireland. His mother was born in England. We are all British and not American citizens.

Now, there was some doubt in William Joyce's mind about his status. Throughout his life when he was filling in official forms he was apt to give his birthplace as Ireland or England, although he had a birth certificate which gave it as Brooklyn. But his disquiet was vague. In the statement he made to the Intelligence officers on his arrest he expressed himself uncertainly.

> I understand, though I have no documents to prove my statement, that my father was American by naturalization at the time of my birth, and I believe he lost his American citizenship later through failing to renew it, because we left America in 1909 when I was three years old. We were generally counted as British subjects during our stay in Ireland and England. I was in Ireland from 1909 till 1921, when I came to England. We were always treated as British during the period of my stay in England, whether we were or not.

But when his defence counsel began to outline his case there was not the faintest doubt about it: William Joyce had not been born a British subject. Documents were brought into court which showed that Michael Joyce had become an American citizen in 1894, twelve years before the birth of William at 1377 Herkimer Street, Brooklyn. In 1909 he had travelled back to England on an American passport. When he and his wife had oscillated between Lancashire and Galway during the First World War they had had to register under the Aliens Act 1915. An old man gave evidence, who had known Michael Joyce all his life. On Joyce's advice this witness had gone to America, worked as a civil engineer, and taken American citizenship, but he had returned to Great Britain during the First World War and had been greatly inconvenienced by his alien status. He spoke of a visit to Mrs Joyce, who was known as Queenie, and who seems to have been very well liked, at her house in a Lancashire town. They had exchanged commiserations because they both had to report all their movements to the police. His cracked old voice evoked a picture of two people cosily grumbling together over their cup of good strong tea thirty years ago.

William's brother Quentin went into the witness-box. There passed between him and the man in the dock a nod and a smile of pure love. One realized that life in this strange family must sometimes have been great fun. But it evidently had not been fun lately. Quentin told the court that his father had died in 1941, shortly after the house in which he had lived for eighteen years had been destroyed by a bomb, and his mother had died in 1944. Out of the wreckage of the house there had been recovered a few boxes full of papers, but none had any bearing on the question of the family's nationality, and there was a reason for that. Michael Joyce had told young Quentin, when he was ten years old, that he and all the family were American citizens but had bade him never to speak of it, and had in later years often reiterated this warning. Finally, in 1934, the boy, who was then sixteen, had seen him burn a number of papers, including what appeared to be an American passport. He had given a reason for what he was doing, but the witness was not required to repeat it. The date suggested what that reason may have been. By that time the police knew William Joyce as a troublesome instigator of street fighting and attacks on Communists and Jews, and in November 1934 Joyce was prosecuted, together with Sir Oswald Mosley and two other Fascists, on a charge of riotous assembly at Worthing; and though this prosecution failed, it indicated a serious attempt by the authorities to rid themselves of the nuisance of Fascist-planned disorder. Michael Joyce had every reason to fear that, if the police ever got an inkling of his secret, they would deport his son and not improbably the whole family.

Now it seemed as impossible to convict William Joyce as it had been, when the prosecution was opening its case, to imagine him acquitted. The child of a naturalized American citizen, born after his father's naturalization, is an American citizen by birth. Therefore William Joyce owed the King of England no allegiance such as arises out of British nationality. It seemed he must go scot free. He had committed no offence whatsoever in becoming a naturalized German subject on 26 September

1940. That would have been high treason had he been a British subject, for a British subject is forbidden by law to become the naturalized subject of an enemy country in wartime. But when he took out his naturalization papers in Germany he was an American citizen, and even the American Government could not have questioned his action, being then at peace with Germany, which did not declare war on the United States until 11 December 1941. It followed, then, that his broadcasting was, if only his nationality had to be considered, an offence against nobody. After 26 September 1940 he had been a good German working for the fatherland. But our law is not really as arbitrary as all that. Allegiance is not exacted by the Crown from a subject simply because the Crown is the Crown. The idea of the divine right of kings is a comparatively modern vulgarity. According to tradition and logic, the state gives protection to all men within its confines, and in return exacts their obedience to its laws; and the process is reciprocal. When men within the confines of the state are obedient to its laws they have a right to claim its protection. It is a maxim of the law, quoted by Coke in the sixteenth century, that 'protection draws allegiance and allegiance draws protection' (*protectio trahit subjectionem, et subjectio protectionem*). It was laid down in 1608, by reference to the case of Sherley, a Frenchman who had come to England and joined in a conspiracy against the King and Queen, that such a man 'owed to the King obedience, that is, so long as he was within the King's protection'. That is fair enough; and indeed very fair, if the limitations which were applied to this proposition were considered. For in Hale's *History of the Pleas of the Crown*, in the seventeenth century, it was written:

> Because as the subject hath his protection from the King and his laws, so on the other side the subject is bound by his allegiance to be true and faithful to the King. And hence it is, that if an alien enemy come into this kingdom hostilely to invade it, if he be taken, he shall be dealt with as an enemy, but not as a traitor, because he violates no trust nor allegiance. But if an alien, the subject of a foreign prince in amity with the King, live here, and enjoy the benefit of the King's protection, and commit a treason, he shall be judged and executed, as a traitor, for he owes a local allegiance.

There could be no doubt whatsoever that William Joyce owed that kind of allegiance. He had certainly enjoyed the protection of the English law for some thirty years preceding his departure to Germany. The lawyers for the defence, in proving that he did not owe the natural kind of allegiance which springs from British birth, had found themselves under the necessity of disproving beyond all doubt that he owed this other acquired kind; and there were the two damning sentences in his statement: 'We were generally counted as British subjects during our stay in Ireland and England. . . . We were always treated as British during the period of my stay in England whether we were or not.' Thus, though an alien, William Joyce owed the Crown allegiance and was capable of committing treason against it. Again he was heading for conviction. But not for certain. There was a definition of the law which was likely to help him.

In 1707 an assembly of judges laid it down that

> if such alien seeking the Protection of the Crown having a Family and Effects here should during a War with his Native Country go thither and there Adhere to the King's Enemies for the purpose of Hostility, He might be dealt with as a Traitor. For he came and settled here under the Protection of the Crown. And though his Person was removed for a time, his Effects and Family continued still under the same Protection.

Now, the letter of this judgement did not apply to William Joyce. He had taken his wife with him to Germany, and by that marriage he was childless. He had two children by a former marriage, but they were in the care of their mother and did not enter into this case. The effects he possessed when he quitted England were of such a trifling nature that it would be fairer to regard them as abandoned rather than as left under the protection of the Crown. Had he retained any substantial property in the country he would not have had to avail himself of the provisions of the Poor Prisoner's Defence Act. But he was within the sphere of the spirit of the judgement. Joyce disappeared from England at some time between 29 August 1939, when he issued an order dissolving the National Socialist League, the Fascist organization of which he was the head, and 18 September, when he entered the service of the German radio. He was the holder of a

British passport; it was part of his lifelong masquerade as a British subject. He had declared on the application papers that he had been born in Galway, and had not 'lost the status of British subject thus acquired'. He obtained this passport on 6 July 1933, and there is perhaps some significance in that date. He had become a member of the British Fascists in 1923, when he was seventeen, but had left this organization after two years, to become later an active member of the Conservative party. In January 1933 Hitler seized power, and later in the year Mosley formed the British Union of Fascists, which William Joyce joined. This passport was, like all British passports, valid for five years. When July 1938 came round he let it lapse, but applied on 24 September 1938 for a renewal for the customary period of one year; and there is, perhaps, some significance in that date also, for the Munich Agreement was signed on 29 September. The next year he was careful not to let it lapse. He made an application for renewal over a month before its expiry on 24 August 1939, and there was certainly some significance in that date, for war broke out on 3 September. Each of these renewals was dated as if the application had been made when the passport expired. So when William Joyce went to Germany he was the holder of a British passport which was valid until the beginning of July 1940. That was why the third count of an indictment charged him with committing high treason by broadcasting between 'the eighteenth day of September 1939, and on divers other days thereafter, and between that day and the second day of July 1940, being then to wit, on the said several days, a person owing allegiance to our lord the King'. It was, in fact, the case for the prosecution that a person obtaining a passport placed himself thereby under the protection of the Crown and owed it allegiance until the passport expired.

No ruling on the point existed, because no case of treason involving temporary allegiance had been tried during the comparatively recent period when passports, in their modern sense, have been in use, so the judge had to make a new ruling; and for one sultry afternoon and a sultrier morning the prosecuting and defending counsel bobbed up and down in front of the bench, putting the arguments for and against the broadening of the law by inclusion of this modern circumstance. People with legal minds were entranced, and others slept. Joyce enjoyed this part of the trial very much, and frequently passed down to his counsel notes that were characteristically odd. Like all prisoners in the dock, he had been given octavo sheets to write on, and could certainly have had as many as he wanted. But when he wrote a note he tore off irregularly shaped pieces and covered them with grotesquely large handwriting; so large that it could be read by people sitting in the gallery. One ended with the words, 'but it is not important'. His enjoyment of the argument was not unnatural in one who loved complications, for no stage of it was simple. Much depended on the nature of a passport, and this had never been defined by the law, for a passport has been different things at different times and has never been merely one thing at a time. It was originally a licence given by the Crown to a subject who wished to leave the realm, an act as a rule prohibited because it deprived the King of a man's military services; but it was also a licence given to an alien to travel through the realm; and it was a pass given to soldiers going home on leave, or paupers discharged from a hospital. Through the ages it changed its character to a demand by the issuing state that the person and property of one of its subjects shall be respected by other states when he travels in their realms; a voucher of his respectability, demanded by the states he intends to visit, as a precaution against crime and political conspiracy; and a source of revenue to the states, which charged heavily for such permits. Of its protective nature in our day there can be little doubt, since the preamble on every passport announces that 'we [the Foreign Secretary of the day] request and require in the Name of Her Majesty all those whom it may concern to allow the bearer to pass freely without let or hindrance, and to afford him or her every assistance and protection of which he or she may stand in need'. In 1905 the Lord Chief Justice of that day, Lord Alverstone, defined a passport as 'a document, issued in the name of a Sovereign, on the responsibility of a Minister of the Crown to a named individual, intended to be presented to the governments of foreign nations and to be used for that individual's protection as a British subject in foreign countries'.

It is a strange thing that many people found something distasteful in this argument that William Joyce, an alien by birth who had acquired a temporary and local allegiance, did not lose it when he left England to take service with the Nazis because he took his British passport with him. They did not reflect on what would have followed from the rejection of this argument. If it had been established that a temporary allegiance could not be carried over by an alien to the Continent, that he divested himself of it by the mere act of passing beyond the three-mile territorial limits, then an alien who was resident in England and held a British passport (as sometimes happens in the case of aliens who have rendered special services to England) could pop across the Channel, conspire with an enemy of England at Calais, and pop back again, not only once but hundreds of times, and never be tried for treason, because at three miles from Dover he lost his duty of allegiance.

Joyce's counsel also argued that his client's passport could give him no protection, because he had acquired it by a false statement; yet it was hard to see how it could fail to protect him until the fraud was discovered and the passport was withdrawn. Supposing that William Joyce had fallen out with the Germans during 1940 and had become a civil internee, he could have called on the assistance of the Swiss Embassy in Berlin, as Switzerland was 'the protective power' appointed to safeguard the interests of Britons in hostile territory during wartime.

All this filigree work delighted the little man in the dock, who watched his lawyers with a cynical brightness, as if he were interested in seeing whether they could get away with all this nonsense but had no warmer concern with the proceedings. He showed no special excitement, only a continuance of amused curiosity, when on the third day of the trial, at the end of the morning, the judge announced that he would give his ruling on these legal submissions after the luncheon interval; and at two o'clock he returned to the dock with his usual eccentric excess of military smartness and his sustained tight-lipped derisiveness. The judge announced that 'beyond a shadow of doubt' William Joyce had owed allegiance to the Crown of this country when he applied for his passport, and that nothing had happened to put an end to that allegiance during the period when the passport was valid. In other words, he ruled that a person holding a British passport owed allegiance to the Crown even when he was outside the realm. This ruling made it quite certain that William Joyce was going to be sentenced to death.

If the sentence were carried out he would die the most completely unnecessary death that any criminal has ever died on the gallows. He was the victim of his own and his father's life-long determination to lie about their nationality. For had he not renewed his English passport, and had he left England for Germany on the American passport which was rightfully his, no power on earth could have touched him. As he became a German citizen by naturalization before America came into the war, he could never have been the subject of prosecution under the American laws of treason.

It is not easy to understand why the family practised this imposture. Michael Joyce is an enigmatic figure. Since he loved England, it would have been more natural for him to emigrate to England than to America. There were, of course, some pro-English Irish who went to America to act as informers on the anti-English Irish, who were at that time fomenting the Fenian and other separatist movements. It is said that Michael Joyce was a candid and honourable man, but even such could, even against their own wish, be entangled in the fierce intrigues and counter-intrigues of those days. It is very difficult to see why, when Michael Joyce returned to England and found his American citizenship such a burden that he warned his children to keep it a deadly secret,

he never took the simple steps which would have readmitted him to British nationality. It would have cost him
only a few pounds, and he was in those years well-to-do.
It cannot have been the legal technicalities which baffled
him; his wife's brother was a solicitor. The official resistance to the process was not great. Can Michael Joyce
have feared to remind either the British or the American
Government of his existence? Had he once been involved
in some imbroglio and got a black mark against his name?
Was he working his passage home when he gained the
good opinion of the Royal Irish Constabulary? There is
probably nobody alive now who knows. All that we can
be sure of is that the story was certainly incredibly complicated. Nothing was simple in that world of espionage
and counter-espionage.

William Joyce was being sentenced to death because
his father had tried to save him from what must have been
a lesser danger; and sentence was passed on him in a terrible way, because nobody in court felt any emotion at all.
People wanted Joyce to pay the proper legal penalty for
his treason, but not because they felt any personal hatred
against him. They wanted to be sure that in any other war
this peculiarly odious form of treachery, which invaded
the ears of frightened people, would be discouraged before
it began, and that was about the limit of their interest in
the matter. At no other such trial have the spectators, as
soon as the jury went out to consider their verdict and the
judge retired from the bench and the prisoner was taken
down to the cells, got up from their seats and strolled
about and chattered as if they were at a theatre between
the acts. At no other such trial have the jury come back

from considering their verdict looking as if they had been out for a cup of tea. Yet their verdict was that he was guilty on the third count in his indictment: of broadcasting for the Nazis between 18 September 1939 and 2 July 1940. He was acquitted on the charge of becoming a naturalized German in September 1940, because he had every right to do that, being an American citizen; and, as for the other indictment, he had had every right to broadcast for the Nazis once he was a German. But he was found guilty on the charge of broadcasting for the Nazis while he was still holding a British passport, and that was high treason, and carried the penalty of death. And at no other such trial has the judge assumed the black cap—which is not a cap at all but a piece of black cloth that an attendant lays across his wig—as if it were in fact just a piece of black cloth laid across his wig. He spoke the words of the sentence of death reverently, and they were awful, as they always must be: 'William Joyce, the sentence of the Court upon you is, that you be taken from this place to a lawful prison, and thence to a place of execution, and that you be there hanged by the neck until you are dead; and that your body be afterwards buried within the precincts of the prison in which you shall have been confined before your execution. And may the Lord have mercy on your soul.'

But the effect of these words was, on this uniquely shallow occasion, soon dissipated. It was indeed pitiful when Joyce was asked if he wanted to make a statement before sentence was passed on him, and he shook his head, the hungry and inordinate voice in him at last defeated. He had been even more pitiful earlier in the trial, when the judge had warned the jury to consider very carefully their verdict because a person found guilty must be sentenced to death, for he had put up his hand and touched his neck with a look of wonder. That he deserved pity was noted by the intellect; pity was not felt. Nor was anybody in the court very much moved by the extreme courage with which he bore himself, though that was remarkable. He listened to the sentence with his head high, gave one of his absurd stiff bows, and ran down to the cells, smiling and waving to his brother and his friends, acting gaiety without a flaw. Such a performance would once have moved us, but not then. All had changed. Even a trial for a capital offence was then quite different from what it had been before the war, when the spectators were living in a state of security, and the prisoner was an exceptionally unfortunate person who had strayed into a district not generally visited, perhaps for lack of boldness. But every man and woman who attended Joyce's trial had at some time during the past six years been in danger of undeserved death or pain, and had shown, or seen others showing, great courage. William Joyce could not make any claim on them by being pitiful and brave. He could not arouse their interest because it was exceptional to meet violent death, since he was in the dock by reason of failure to acquit himself well when that had been their common destiny. So they turned away from him and left the court as if it had been a cinema or concert. But in the dark corridor a woman said: 'I am glad his mother's dead. She lived near us in Dulwich. She was a sweet little lady, a tiny little woman. I often used to stand with her in the fish queue. In fact, that's how I met her. One day after the blitz had been very bad I said something about that blasted Lord Haw-Haw, and someone said, "Hush, that's his mother right beside you," and I felt dreadful. But she only said—but she was ever so Irish, and I can't speak like she did—"Never mind, my dear, I'm sure you didn't mean it unkindly."' This story recalled the lilt of affection of the old man in the witness-box when he had spoken of having tea with Queenie.

The dark corridor passed to a twilit landing. Down a shadowed staircase the band of Fascists were descending, tears shining on their astonished faces. Joyce's brother walked slowly, his eyes that were soft and brown like a cow's now narrow and wet, and the slight blond solicitor just behind him. There was a block, and for a minute the crowd all stood still. The solicitor plucked at Quentin Joyce's jacket and said kindly, 'This is just what he expected, you know.' 'Yes,' said his brother, 'I know it's just what he expected.' The crowd moved on, but after it had gone down a few steps the solicitor plucked at the young man's jacket again and said, 'It's the appeal that matters, you know,' and Quentin said, 'Yes, I know. The appeal's everything.'

At the counter where the spectators had to collect their umbrellas and coats, a jurywoman was saying good-bye to one of her colleagues. They were shaking hands warmly and expressing hopes that they would meet again. They might have been people parting at the end of a cruise. Jostling them were the Fascists, waiting for their raincoats, garments which those of their kind affect in all weathers, in imitation of Hitler. The young man who looked like a gipsy held his head down. Heavy tears were hanging on his long black lashes. He and his friends still looked amazed. They had wanted people to die by violence, but they had not expected the lot to fall on any of their own number.

Another dark and passionate young man was accosted by a reporter, and he cried out in rage that he had been four years in Brixton Jail under Security Regulation 18b, all for patriotism, and he had come out to see the persecution of the finest patriot of all. His black eyes rolled and blazed about him. It did not do. About him were standing people who had been in the Dieppe expedition, at Arnhem, in submarines, in prison camps; even the women knew about fear, had been, perhaps, on the Gestapo list of persons to be arrested immediately after the Germans conquered England. There was this new universality of horrible experience, this vast common martyrdom, which made it no use to play execution as if it were a trump card.

The little band of Fascists gathered together in a knot by the door, and after they had wiped their faces, and composed themselves, they went into the street. In the open space in front of the building was a line of parked cars, and behind them stood a crowd of silent people. The Fascists walked away from this crowd, down a street that narrowed and lost itself in a network of alleys. Nobody followed them, but they began to hurry. By the time they got into the shelter of the alleys, they were almost running.

CHAPTER 2

The fight between the Crown and William Joyce was waged throughout four months and all across London. It began in a golden September in the Old Bailey, came up again during bright November in another damaged building, the Royal Courts of Justice, and then went to the House of Lords, where he made his last stand in the precincts of Westminster Palace, which, still hugger-mugger within from bomb damage, looked across the river through December mists at one of the most moving memorials of the blitz, St Thomas's Hospital, still treating the sick, but itself architecturally sick after much bombing.

For a week the trial imposed its routine on St Stephen's. In the morning the spectators, either journalists or the faithful in their Hitler raincoats with their look of Irishry and their wild unhappiness, went up the stone staircase to a lobby full of gossiping lawyers, outside the chamber where the Lords were meeting temporarily because they had given their chamber over to the Commons, whose home had been damaged by a bomb. They were then taken in hand by the attendants of the House of Lords, a body of spare and anonymous-looking men in ordinary white-tie evening dress, with the silver-gilt badge of the Royal Arms at their waists, under the supervision of a most elegant retired general, whose appearance and manners would have delighted Ouida. They shepherded all the pressmen and the prisoner's friends into the Royal Gallery, a hall conceived and executed in the brownest style of Victorian interior decoration, which held that everything rich, and not just plum cake, should be dark. On the wall, strips of mulberry and gold brocade divide vast blackish frescoes in which a welter of arms and legs set at every angle round a few war horses suggests military effort, dingy gilded figures of kings and queens guard the doors, and in an alcove two togaed figures, quite black, though obviously they represent persons belonging to the white race, make expansive political gestures of a meliorist type. Brightness came from only one object. In a corner there is a glass-covered display table lit from within in which there lies a book inscribed with the names of peers and their sons who were killed in war, but not the last war, the one before that, of 1914 to 1918. Each day a fresh page is turned.

Every morning, while we waited, a bishop in black robes and huge white lawn sleeves hovered at the door of the chamber in which the Lords sit, ready to go in and say the prayers which open the day's session, until an attendant cried, 'Make way for the Mace!' and we were all ordered off the strip of oatmeal matting which runs across the tiled floor. Then a procession came in, never quite at ease, it was so small and had never had enough start to get up the processional spirit. The Serjeant-at-Arms came first, carrying the great golden pepper-pot on a stalk which is the Mace. Another attendant followed, carrying a purse embroidered with the Royal Arms, representing the Great Seal. Then came the Lord Chancellor, Lord Jowitt, superb in his white full-bottomed wig, its curls lying in rows on his shoulders, and wearing a long black silk gown with a train carried by an attendant. He carried between the forefinger and thumb of each hand his black velvet cap. The ritual is not mere foolishness. The procession and the symbols are a mnemonic guide to the constitutional functions of the House of Lords, and are part of a complicated convention into which most of the legislative and judicial activities of Parliament fit conveniently enough, and which nobody would much care to rewrite, in view of the trickiness of procedure.

While prayers were said by the Lords we stood and waited. Around the room ran a shiny quilted red-leather bench, but nobody ever sat on it except Joyce's solicitor, a man whose destiny should be noted. He was a fragile creature, almost a dwarf, and he was much respected in his profession. He looked older than he had at the first trial, and indeed, he shortly afterwards became ill and died. It is not easy to estimate what it must have cost him to have conducted for four months, with an efficiency remarked on by all the lawyers who followed the case, the defence of one whose opinions were unattractive to him and whom he had not chosen to defend, simply having been allotted to him under the Poor Persons Defence Act. He conferred, his appearance of fatigue daily increasing, with William Joyce's brother Quentin, who also looked much older. At the Old Bailey he had been a fresh-faced boy but now he might have been getting on for forty. Deep furrows were grooving his forehead, and his eyes were small and sunken, and, in the mornings, red with weeping. With him were always two friends. One was tall Angus MacNab, who was plainly the eccentric, nonconforming gentleman, so often, as the great American Henry Adams so memorably complained, produced by the British people. The other was a young Fascist of Scottish origin, whose remote blue-grey eyes showed that he had escaped from the world into dreams, not vaguer and kinder than the existence round us, as the dreams of most people are, but harsher and more troubled. All three were lifted to the heights of dignity by their grief for William, whom they were mourning as early Christians might have mourned a brother about to go into the arena.

There was a real cult around the little man. Some rumour of it had been spreading abroad since the trial began. The City of London greatly respected a certain aged stockbroker, belonging to a solid Scottish family, who conducted a large business with the strictest probity and was known to his friends as a collector of silver and glass and a connoisseur of wine. He had a beautiful house, kept for him by his sister, a tall and handsome maiden lady given to piety and good works, whose appearance was made remarkable by an immense knot of hair twisted on the nape of her neck in the mid-Victorian way. The old man's last years were afflicted by a depressing illness, during which he formed a panic dread of Socialism, and for this reason he fell under the influence of Sir Oswald Mosley, to whom he gave a considerable amount of money and whose followers he often entertained. This is a sad thought when it is remembered that many of those followers were very ugly scoundrels; one was prosecuted for living on the earnings of a prostitute. The old man had a special fondness for William Joyce, who, being a lively, wisecracking, practical-joking little creature, as well as intelligent, was able to cheer up an invalid; and after his death his sister, who carried on all his enthusiasms, treated Joyce like a son. She let him use her country house as a meeting-place for the heads of his organization, and entertained him there so often that it was one of the first places searched by the police at the outbreak of war when they found that Joyce had left his home.

This woman, then over eighty and crippled by a painful disease, rose from her bed to travel up to London, an apocalyptic figure, tall and bowed, the immense knot of hair behind her head shining snow-white, and went to see William Joyce in prison. She returned weeping but uplifted by his courage and humility and his forgiveness of all his enemies and his faith in the righteousness of his cause. To all those whom she especially loved she sat down and wrote letters describing her visit to this holy and persecuted man which truly might have wrung the heart, and she followed them with copies of the letters that he wrote to her from prison, in which he said that he knew well that the issue of his trial might be against him but was not dismayed, since he could think of no better death than dying for his faith. These pretensions on behalf of a man who worked to enable Hitler and Göring to set up Nazism in England were obviously fantastic, and there was only a minute and crazed fraction of the population which would have accepted them at that time. His luck at other times would have been variable. There is always some market for

Messiahs, but some (and surely he was one, and that was his tragedy) are never quoted very high.

Presently we were let into the chamber where Joyce was to be tried, and found ourselves in a twilit space under a gallery, quite close to the barristers sitting in their wigs and gowns, who were silhouetted against the brightness of the lit chamber beyond. Their faces turned on one of their number who stood speaking to the Lord Chancellor who, dressed in his robes, was sitting at a table in the broad aisle which ran down the middle of the chamber, together with four old judges who were dressed in lounge suits and swathed in steamer rugs. There was, of course, not enough fuel available at that time to heat the place, and it was bitterly cold. In the farthest corner of the darkness under the gallery, with four warders to guard him, was William Joyce, his face altered by new wisdom and yellowish prison pallor. Like his brother he had changed greatly since the trial at the Old Bailey. There he had seemed meanly and repulsively ugly, but at the Law Courts, where his first appeal was heard, he was not so. He was puny and colourless, but his face had an amusing, pleasant, even prettyish character. It was not good-looking, but it could be imagined that people who knew him well would find it easy to believe him far better-looking than he was. This alteration was due in part to improvement in his health. He had arrived in England from Germany shabby and tousled and sickly, pulled down by the hardships he had endured when he was on the run between his last broadcast and his capture by English troops, and by the wound in his leg he had sustained when he was arrested. During his imprisonment he had eaten and slept well, and was among those prisoners who had put on weight while under sentence of death. But he looked better because he had sat at the Old Bailey with the right side of his face turned towards spectators, while at the Law Courts it was the left side we saw; and a deep scar ran from the lobe of his right ear to the right corner of his mouth, destroying the contour of the cheek. There was a certain mystery about this scar. His friends were reticent. At the time he suffered the injury he was a student at Battersea Polytechnic, and it was then believed by his fellow students and at least one of the staff that he had either been slashed with a razor or mauled with the leg of a chair by a Communist in a street fight arising from a British Fascist meeting. But he had sustained the wound in the General Election of 1924, when defending the platform at a Tory meeting in Lambeth from an ugly rush; and it was perhaps embarrassing to the anti-Semite Joyce that the Tory candidate he had defended was Jewish: Mr Jack Lazarus. In any case it added to the handicaps already laid on him by his smallness and oddity.

In the Law Courts one saw what he would have been like had he not been, on some occasion, cut to the bone; and one saw the humour nothing had taken from him. Prisoners in the dock laugh more freely than is generally imagined; judicial jokes which so often annoy the newspaper reader are to them an opportunity for relaxation. But Joyce's amusement at his own appeal was more subtle than that. One of the judges on the bench was most picturesquely comic in appearance and might have come straight out of the *commedia dell'arte*, and him William Joyce watched with delight. The legal arguments he followed with an unusual detachment; once nodding in approval when a point was decided against him.

But here at the House of Lords he had endured a further change. He still followed the legal argument with a bright eye. But the long contemplation of death had given him a dignity and refinement that he had lacked before. It could be recognized when he turned his eyes on the spectators who paused to look at him before they went up to their seats in the gallery. At the Old Bailey he had soon come to recognize those who were sitting through the whole trial, and it had entertained him to catch their eyes and stare them out. At the Court of Appeal he gave the spectators an inquisitive and gentler eye. That he was a civilized man, however aberrant, was somehow clear before our eyes, and mournful. At the House of Lords he had gone past compassion, looking at us from a territory where clocks kept another time than ours, and listening to the striking of an hour that had not yet struck for us. A steep staircase led up to the gallery, where one sat under the huge shapes of Edwardian frescoes dedicated to the obsessive devotion felt by the British aristocracy for the horse. That had been traceable outside in the Royal Gallery, for in the blackish frescoes the horses had been the only living creatures which in a scene of catastrophe had remained the right way up. Within, the tribute was even more ardent. The fresco beside the gallery had the word 'Hospitality' written underneath it, and showed a lot of people in the old Covent Garden Wagnerian costumes on a Covent Garden abbey set, all of them welcoming a man who, oddly enough, was riding in on a horse. But that was not really hospitality. They were plainly glad to see him because he was riding a horse. Behind the gallery the word 'Generosity' was written under a fresco showing a horseman refraining from killing a man lying on the ground, on the advice of his horse, who was turning an elder-statesman muzzle toward him. There was a horse in every fresco except one, in which there was a divine person instead.

At the end of the chamber were the two royal thrones—the Queen's carefully built a little lower than the King's—raised on a dais with two steps. In front of the thrones, on the floor of the house, was the Woolsack, a red, stuffed pouffe on which the Mace was lying; during normal sessions of the House the Lord Chancellor sits on it. On the floor of the House there was also a table covered with very new and bright red leather, at which a clerk in wig and gown sat throughout the trial, doing some official task not to be comprehended by the uninitiated, cutting up paper with scissors as if he were preparing for paper games at a very large children's party. Running lengthwise on each side of the floor were the three rows of benches on which the peers sat, and there some were sitting. But they were no part of Joyce's trial, they were spectators like the rest of us. For though a prisoner appeals to the whole House of Lords for judgement on his case, the House refers the matter to a small committee of judges, drawn from a panel of law lords. In Joyce's case these judges numbered four, with the Lord Chancellor as a fifth. The counsel addresses this committee not on the floor of the House but from the bar of the House, which was just under the gallery where we were all sitting. To follow the case we had to listen to a thin thread of sound emitted by invisible speakers under our feet. Quentin Joyce had to partake in this general inconvenience and surely Hell could provide no greater torture than to follow a brother's destiny in these conditions.

The lawyers swung their argument back and forth for four days. Mid-mornings, a stately attendant glided across the scene of baronial pomp bearing a very common little tea-tray for the comfort of the shivering judges. Peers dropped in to listen and sat about on the red rep benches, some of their eldest sons exercised their curious right to sit on the steps of the dais beneath the thrones. One peer lived through a most painful moment of his life during the trial. Following an intricate point, he ran his finger thoughtfully up and down behind the lapel of his coat, but suddenly stopped. A look of agony passed over his face, and he turned back the lapel. He had found a moth hole and for a long time was unable to think about William Joyce. These were the days of clothes coupons.

The story became more ironical each time it was restated. Here was a man who was being strangled by the sheer tortuousness of his family destiny. He was an American by birth who, by his father's wish, had pretended all his life to be British. Why? In the third trial, as in the first and the second, that question was never answered. It had become more perplexing as more knowledge about William Joyce had come into currency. He had stood as a candidate at a London County Council election and had at that time had to declare that he was a British subject; and that false declaration might have brought on him, had he been elected, a fine of £50 for every occasion on which he had sat on the council. Why did the father—who loved his eldest son very dearly, and must have acquired in the course of his life as a close friend of the British Police Government of Ireland a reasonable notion of the law's view of such capers as his son's—keep his own and his family's status a close secret, as if their lives depended on it? Perhaps they did, but it is not likely. This mysterious imposture was bringing Joyce closer and closer to the gallows as we listened to the thread of sound beneath our feet.

The legal content of each of Joyce's trials was slightly different: different as, say, three performances of the same concerto by the same conductor and the same soloist but by three different orchestras. At the Old Bailey the fantastic novelty of the case, and the disturbing presence of the Judas whose voice we all knew so well, had overwhelmed the court and proceedings were rough-hewn. In the Court of Appeal the performance was more delicate. The contentions on which Joyce's counsel asked the Court of Appeal to reverse the verdict returned at the Old Bailey were four, and they were by that time strictly lawyers' meat. The argument which impressed the public most was in fact the least respectable: that a man who obtained a passport by fraud as Joyce had done could not owe allegiance in return for the protection he derived from it. This is not horse-sense; for it means that a man who fraudulently obtained a British passport would be better off than a man who obtained it legally. He would get protection without having to give allegiance. It is not easy to imagine why the public conceived tenderness for this argument, and perhaps less would have been felt had it been realized on what grounds Joyce's counsel justified it. First, he claimed, that protection which attracted allegiance was not protection *de facto* but protection *de jure*, not actual protection but the legal right to it, and therefore a man who obtained a passport by fraud and was not getting its protection lawfully could use it to what benefit was possible and then walk off whistling. The other argument was that the moment the holder of a passport committed treason the power which granted the passport withdrew its protection, so the whole transaction regarding the document was null and void. One of the three judges at the Court of Appeal, the one who looked like a character in the *commedia dell'arte*, thought little of this point, and to show it puffed out his cheeks and spouted out air through his leathery old lips dolphin-wise, while William Joyce watched him with amusement in which there was some affection.

Here in the House of Lords the performance became even quicker, finer, subtler, and Joyce enjoyed himself thoroughly. When the four old judges had a passage with counsel, it was not only, presumably, great law. It was also as good entertainment as first-class tennis. All of them had supremely good minds, as well as the physiological luck that makes a man able to go on through the seventies into the eighties doing what he has done all his life better and better, even though he may not be able to address himself to new tasks or work continuously. The voice of each old man was characteristic enough to be easily identifiable, and often, in the quieter moments, recalled what was generally known about him. One among them had a small manor-house set in a forest lying under the Wiltshire Downs. He lived there with a wife much younger than himself, who was perhaps the most celebrated professional horsewoman in England. At night he sat at his end of the table surrounded by his pupils, who had come to learn from him the subtlest mysteries of the law, and she sat at her end surrounded by her pupils, who had come to learn from her the subtlest mysteries of fox-hunting and horse-breaking. The two groups were hardly able to communicate with each other, owing to the extreme specialization of each, but as there is nothing so civilizing as scholarship and craftsmanship which have not lost touch with life, the judge and his wife lived together in the most agreeable amity.

It was not fair. Here were these old men, full of honours because of an intellectual distinction which Joyce shared with them to a considerable degree, otherwise he would not have felt the admiration for them he expressed to those who visited him in prison. Here was the Palace of Westminster, built to house and glorify a system which he would have liked to adorn. Every morning he was taken into court by his guard while the public was still waiting for admission, and on all four days he owned to his warders, laughing at himself yet quite in earnest, how much he enjoyed making this ceremonial entrance into the Mother of Parliaments. Had he been able to range freely round the pompous halls and corridors, he would have seen the reason for the pomp far better than most visitors. With real reverence he would have bent over the glass-covered display table and looked at the book inscribed with the names of the peers and their sons who had fallen in the First World War; the procession of the Mace into the House of Lords would have been recognized by him as having a meaning. His relationship with the State might have been perfect, had it not been that he had made one stipulation which could not be fulfilled. He wanted to govern, not to be governed; and that, for reasons which were not fair, was quite impossible.

That became visible as the trial came to its conclusion, which was painfully protracted. This third trial began on a

Monday, and it looked as if the verdict would be given on Thursday afternoon. At one o'clock on Thursday counsel had finished their arguments, and the Lord Chancellor dismissed the court and bade it reassemble at three. Joyce's brother Quentin and his friend the Scottish Fascist rose miserably and went off to look for some lunch. This was not too easy to get, for in those days, just after the War, people lunched early, and in few restaurants would there be tables free or much food left. Outside the Houses of Parliament everyone knew who they were and eyed them with wonder, aware of their peculiar grief, their terrifying sympathies. They crossed the street and passed into the crowds of Whitehall, and there they became two young men in raincoats among ten thousand such.

When everyone had reassembled, the Lord Chancellor announced that the judges required more time to consider their verdict, and dismissed the court again until Tuesday morning. Tears stood in Quentin Joyce's eyes, and he and his friends pressed forward to get out of the hated place as soon as might be. But the attendants held all of us back, and we stood together at the head of the steep stairs, looking down on William Joyce as he was marched out among the four policemen on his way back to jail. Now his courage was impressive. At the Old Bailey he had behaved well, but under a simple though supreme danger, of which most of those present had some experience. But now he was doing something more difficult. He had lived four months under the threat of death, and now he had not heard the decisive sentence he had been braced to hear, and after this disabling moment had had to walk through a crowd of his enemies, a little ill-made man surrounded by four drilled giants. He held his chin high and picked his feet up, as the sergeant-majors say, and though he held his chin so very high that his face was where the top of his head ought to have been and though his feet flapped on his weak ankles, his dignity was not destroyed, but was made idiosyncratic, his very own. It appeared that there could be such a thing as undignified dignity. Yet in that moment when he compelled respect, it became quite clear that he could never have been one of our governors. Even if he had not been a Fascist, if he had been sponsored by the Tory or the Labour or the Liberal party, he would never have been given power.

There was a bar between Joyce and advancement, no matter what he made of himself. He had taken a good degree in English at London University; but that could not be guessed from any of his writings or his speeches, and it is said that he became a coach because his application for posts in schools and colleges met with embarrassed discouragement. Though he had developed his gifts for public speaking in the service of the Conservative party, there had never been any question of any local committee nominating him as Parliamentary candidate. There was some element in him that resisted the cultivation of all his merits. It was even manifest in his body. He was a good rider, a still better swimmer and diver, he fenced, and had tried hard as a featherweight boxer; but his little body looked as if he never cared to exercise it. He seemed mediocre when he was not, perhaps because of some contrary quality, which put people off; an exaggeration amounting to clownishness. For example; he always retained the love of England which he expressed in his boyish letters to the

London University Committee for Military Education; but in after life it led him to make a demand, which struck many of his English acquaintances as a sign of insanity, that any social evening he spent with his friends, even the quietest, should end with the singing of the National Anthem.

When Tuesday came the Press and the Fascists no longer had the Royal Gallery to themselves. It was thronged with Members of Parliament, a comradely and self-assured crowd, happily gossiping on their own stamping-ground and much less respectful to the ceremonies of the place than the Press and the Fascists had been. They had to be pushed off the carpet by the attendants when the Mace and the Lord Chancellor went by, so busy were they exchanging comments on Joyce which were not meant inhumanly but sounded so, because they themselves were in such good health and so unlikely, if things went on as they were going, to be hanged: 'They say he isn't here today.' 'No, if he were acquitted, it would be awkward. They'd want to arrest him immediately on defence-regulation charges, and nobody can be arrested within the Palace of Westminster. They'd have to let him go down the street, and he might get away.' 'Perhaps he's chosen not to come today. Shouldn't blame him.' 'He's very plucky. I saw him at the Old Bailey.' 'So did I. What a queer little fish!' Joyce's brother was standing beside the last speaker, but he seemed not to hear. Both the Fascists and the Pressmen were all preoccupied with the need to dash up into the gallery the minute the signal was given, because the announcement of the verdict would take only a few seconds and might be over before they had climbed the stairs.

The Lord Chancellor and the four judges were sitting around the table at the bar of the House, as they had done every day, but now the red benches were fully occupied, the House was crowded with peers; there seemed so many it was remarkable that nobility had kept its distinction. As the Press and the public took their seats in the gallery, the Lord Chancellor rose and stood silent till there was quietness, and then said, 'I have come to the conclusion that the appeal should be dismissed. In common with the rest of your Lordships, I should propose to deliver my reasons at a later date.' Then the four old judges rose in turn and gave their opinions. While the first was saying 'I agree', Joyce's brother and his friends got up from their seats beside mine in the second row which had been assigned to newspaper agencies and were not now occupied. Suddenly one of the suave attendants was standing beside them and was saying, in a tone of savagery the more terrifying because it was disciplined and was kept low so that the proceedings should not be disturbed, 'You get out of there and go back to the seats where you belong.' This seemed a most brutal way of behaving to men who were listening to a judgement that doomed one whom they loved; for all the judges except one were saying 'I agree', and that meant that Joyce must hang. But on the face of the attendant, and of others who had joined him, there was real fear. Innocent though Quentin Joyce and his friends were, they had become associated with the idea of violence, and from the front of the gallery a violent man could have thrown grenades into the court.

Meanwhile the ceremony went on, affecting in its beauty and its swiftness. The Lord Chancellor moved backward down the floor of the House, in his black robe and curled white wig, the only figure in a historic dress in the assembly, the symbol of the continuing rule of law. He halted at the Woolsack. He stretched out his hands to the peers on each side of the chamber and bade those vote who were content with the judgement. This was the last sad stage of the outnumbering of Joyce by the law. Now scores of judges faced the dock, and he was gone from it. The peers nodded and murmured and raised their hands. At this point a young man with hollow eyes and pinched nose and a muffler round his scrawny neck, who was sitting on the public bench of the gallery among the Negroes and the Hindus, cried out some words which some among us could recognize as Scottish Gaelic, and then proclaimed in English but with a strong northern accent that William Joyce was innocent. Attendants formed a wall around him, but did no more, for fear of interrupting the proceedings. The Negroes beside him expressed horror with rolling eyes; the Hindus looked prim. Joyce's friends threw a glance at him which was at first startled and then snobbish. The interrupter was not one of their sort of Fascist. Meanwhile the Lord Chancellor bade those peers who were not content with the judgement to vote, and there was silence. He declared, 'The contents have it,' and strode from the chamber. The peers streamed after him. The place was empty in a moment.

Quentin Joyce and his friends ran down the stone staircase into the street. They did not look so upset as might have been expected. The man who had shouted made his way out of the gallery without being touched by the attendants, who looked away from him, having taken his measure. In the lobby outside, crowds of Pressmen gathered round him and questioned him and took down his answers, which he delivered with the gasping haste of the evangelist who knows he never keeps his audience long. The elegant general who was in charge of the attendants murmured to the Superintendent of Police, 'I say, do we want this sort of thing, or don't we?' The Superintendent said he thought that the man would probably go away of his own accord if he were left alone. So the eccentric held an audience in the House of Lords, the very considerable crowd that was coming in to take part in the debate on the American loan neatly dividing to avoid disturbing him and joining again, until the Pressmen left him, having insufficiently appreciated the remarkable quality of his utterance. A young reporter asked him, 'But don't you think it mattered that William Joyce betrayed his country?' and he answered, in the accents of Sir Harry Lauder, 'William Joyce didna betray his country. Ye canna say a man betrays his country when he goes abroad to better himself. Millions of people have done that and nobody's accused them of betraying their countries, and that's what William Joyce did. He had a fine position waiting for him in Germany, and he just took it.' Surely this was a mind as fresh as Shaw's. His was a voice which was to be heard again, nearly twenty years later. Strangely enough, it was the only voice lifted on that occasion which was to be heard again.

Down in the street, Quentin Joyce and Angus MacNab and the Scottish Fascist were waiting, eager to speak to the Press, eager to give praise to their martyr. That was why they had not looked so very greatly upset when the appeal was dismissed; they were like the people who, leaving a death-bed so painful to them that they could not have borne to contemplate it for another instant, find relief by flinging themselves into elaborate arrangements for the funeral. Angus MacNab, in his easy and gentlemanly but hollow and eccentric voice, was telling a reporter how calm William Joyce had been when he saw him in prison during the weekend. 'He was in excellent spirits,' he said, his eyes gleaming mystically behind his spectacles, 'and he was discussing, quite objectively, and with all his old brilliance, the psychology of the four judges. He was wonderful. . . . But I must leave you now and go and tell my wife what has happened. My name? Angus MacNab, and please do not spell it M-c-N-a-b. The correct spelling is M-a-c-N-a-b.' And Quentin Joyce was talking freely in his careful voice, which, without being mincing, was more gentlemanly and more English than any English gentleman's voice, because this ambitious and Anglophile family consciously ironed out the Irish brogue from their tongues. Some reporters were asking him to write an article or make some statement about his brother, which he was refusing to do, evidently out of loyalty to some code of family relationships. He seemed to be saying primly that it was for his sister-in-law to tell the story of Joyce when she was free, since a wife was nearer than a brother, and as such must have her rights. It was plain that he and all this group had felt themselves not less but more disciplined than the rest of the world, solid upholders of order. He went on to speak of some demonstration the Fascists would make against the sentence. 'And believe me, there will be plenty of us,' he kept on repeating, while the Scottish Fascist nodded. A year later and for many years after, this man was to insert in the *Daily Telegraph* an 'In Memoriam' notice of William Joyce.

But there were not plenty of them outside Wandsworth Prison on the morning of 3 January, when William Joyce was hanged.

That prison lies in a shabby district in South London, so old-fashioned that it begins to look picturesque to our eyes. It is a mid-Victorian building with a facade of dark stone, inspired by a brooding and passionate misunderstanding of Florentine architecture, and it is divided from the high road by a piece of ground not belonging to the prison, consisting of some cabbage patches and a dispirited nursery garden, planned whimsically, with thin streams trickling under toy bridges and meandering between the blackened stems of frosted chrysanthemums. The prison looks across the high road to a monstrous building—built in the style of a Burgundian château and set in the midst of a bald and sooty park—an endowed school for the children of soldiers and sailors with the curious name of 'The Royal Victoria Patriotic School'. This title had become ironical during the war, for persons who escaped from the occupied countries were detained there, often for dreary weeks, until they had satisfied the authorities that they had not been sent over by the Germans. An avenue runs between the cabbage patches and nursery gardens to the prison's great doorway, which is of green panelled wood with a heavy iron grille at the top, set in a coarse stone archway. A small notice-board hangs on this door; and on it was pinned an announcement that the sentence of death passed on William Joyce was to be carried out that morning. On these occasions there is nothing whatsoever for a spectator to see except at one moment, when a warder comes out of a small door which is cut in the large one, takes down the notice-board, and replaces it after two other notices have been added to the first: one a sheriff's declaration that the prisoner has been hanged, the other a surgeon's declaration that he has examined the prisoner's body and found him to be dead. But about three hundred people gathered to see that minute shred of ceremony.

They gathered while it was still dark and the windows of the cells were yellow in the squat utilitarian buildings which stretched away from the Italian façade—and waited through the dawn till full daylight, stoically bearing the disappointment that the hour of the hanging was at the last moment postponed from eight to nine. Some of those who waited were Pressmen, lamenting that there was no story here; straining figures on the roof of a yellow Movie tone truck set up a tall camera to focus on the notice-board, certain that there would be nothing anywhere else in the scene worth recording. Some people had brought their children, since the little dears, they said, had pestered them to go on this outing. Others were people drawn by personal resentment. An old man told me that he was there because he had turned on the wireless one night during the V-1 blitz when he came back from seeing his grandchildren's bodies in the mortuary and had heard Haw-Haw's voice. 'There he was, mocking me,' he said. There were many soldiers who had strolled out for a little after-breakfast diversion from a nearby demobilization centre. As time went on, all these people danced to keep their feet warm on the frozen earth.

There were some who did not dance. Most of these, however, were not particularly interested in William Joyce.

They were opponents of capital punishment, who would have stood and looked disapproving outside any prison where anybody was being hanged. The most conspicuous of these were two tall and gaunt Scandinavian women dressed in black, who indulged in silent but truculent prayer. Quentin Joyce and his friends were not there; they were attending a requiem mass. During William Joyce's imprisonment he became reconciled to the faith in which he was born. But there must have been many Fascists who would not attend that service, either because they were not Christian or because they were not close enough to Joyce's family to hear of it. Of these only a handful waited outside the prison, and of these only one grieved openly, standing bareheaded, with no effort to hide his tears at the moment of Joyce's hanging. Three others slipped through a gap in the trees of the avenue and stood in the nursery garden, where some rows of cabbage-stalks veiled with frost flanked a rubble rockery, naked with winter, and at that moment they made a shy manifestation of respect. Their bodies betrayed that they had had no military training, and they wore the queer and showy sports clothes affected by Fascists, but they attempted the salute which looks plausible only when performed by soldiers in uniform. It was the poorest send-off for a little man who had always loved a good show and done his best to give one; who, so the prison gossip went, halted on his way to the scaffold, looked down on the violent trembling of his knees, and calmly and cynically smiled.

CHAPTER 3

During the trials there had flowed into the mind of the community a conviction that Joyce had not been guilty of any offence against the law. This was in part due to the inadequate reports of the proceedings, which were all that the Press could find space to publish because it was starved of newsprint. The public read almost nothing about the Joyce trials which was not so brief and disjointed as to be unintelligible, and it came to a conclusion which was summed up in the pubs in some such terms as these:

'Of course he can't be guilty of treason,' they said in the public and in the saloon bars. 'He's a dirty little bastard, but we've no right to hang him, he's an American.' And so it went on. 'A miscarriage of justice,' said the clerk in a government office, handing out a legal document concerning Joyce to an inquirer some months later, 'that's what the verdict was. I hold no brief for the little man, though he was a wonderful speaker. I'm no Fascist, but I always used to listen to him when he spoke up our way by the Great Northern Hospital; but it stands to reason that giving an American a British passport can't change him into an Englishman. A miscarriage of justice, that's what that was.' But this was not a tenable point of view. It had no legal basis, since Joyce had got himself out of the safety of American citizenship by obtaining an English passport. It had no basis in the world of fact, which is sometimes, we must admit, divided from the world of law. William Joyce was not an American in any real sense; and indeed during the war the United States had passed an Act concerning naturalization confirming this view of the reality of citizenship.

In 1940 the United States had declared that persons who owed the sort of allegiance to another country which William Joyce and his father had owed to Great Britain could not retain their American nationality. This declaration was afterwards annulled by a decision of the Supreme Court; but at the time of his trial it held good. Michael Joyce's American naturalization would have been nullified had this Act been in force earlier because he had resided continuously for more than three years in the territory of the foreign state of which he had been a national before he was naturalized a citizen of the United States. William Joyce would have lost his American nationality under the same Act, had it been passed earlier, by his service in the Officers' Training Corps (after the age of eighteen) and by his participation in elections. But there was some merit behind the public's regret that Joyce had been sentenced to death, ill-argued though it was. We were all afraid lest the treatment of Joyce had been determined by our emotions and not by our intellects: that we had been corrupted by our Nazi enemies to the extent of calling vengeance by the name of justice.

The legal profession also showed a discontent with the verdict which was startling. For of the nine judges which had considered the case, one at the Old Bailey, three at the Court of Appeal, and four at the House of Lords, together with the Lord Chancellor, only one (a Lord of Appeal, Lord Porter) had dissented from the verdict of guilty, and he did not fundamentally disagree with his colleagues in their view of allegiance. His objection related to a passage in Mr Justice Tucker's summing-up at the Old Bailey, which he regarded as a misdirection of the jury on a minor technical point. But the lawyers were, like the public, misled by the inadequate press reports. One thinks of lawyers as having a collective consciousness, and becoming aware of all legal proceedings as they happen; but that is child-like faith. 'I'd thought,' one said, 'that Joyce's appeal in the House of Lords was going well for him.' His reason for thinking thus was a remark addressed by the Lord Chancellor to Joyce's counsel: 'Surely the proposition is elementary that allegiance was only due from an alien while he was in this country.' Read out of its context, this sounded like an encouraging invitation to pass on after a point had been proved. Heard, the sentence conveyed with crystalline peevishness that the counsel was hammering home the obvious, and it was followed by the statement, 'The question, surely, is whether there are any exceptions to this rule.'

The lawyers, like the rest of us, had insufficient information, and they also were afraid lest the law had been tainted by revenge, and this they felt sharply and personally, since it was their mystery which was being profaned.

Such scruples were honourable, and it would be an unhealthy community which did not recognize them. But the situation was not simple. A number of people were say-ing, 'William Joyce was a vile man but he should not have been hanged,' and smiled as they said it, claiming to speak in the name of mercy. But they were hypocrites. They were moved by hostility to the law, being destructive by nature.

Nowhere has the law been finally analysed and defined. To make laws is a human instinct which arises as soon as food and shelter have been ensured, among all peo-ples, everywhere. There have been yellow people who have flashed on horseback across continents, apparently too mobile to form customs, apparently preoccupied with slaughter and devastation. There have been black people who have squatted on their haunches through the cen-turies, their customs degenerating to superstition round them. These have been thought by men of other kinds to be without law, but that was an error. Both kinds of society had reached a general agreement as to how to order their lives, and ordained penalties against its violation. But neither they nor any other society could define exactly what they were doing when they were making that agree-ment and ordaining those penalties. Demosthenes said that every rule of law was a discovery and a gift from the gods, and he added that it was also an opinion held by sensible men. Nine hundred years later the great Justinian prefixed that same definition to his *Digest of Laws*, only changing 'gods' to God. Both seemed guilty of paradox, for assuredly men are not gods, and the last thing a god or God could fairly be compared with is a sensible man. Yet pagan and Christian alike realized that the law should be at once the recognition of an eternal truth and the solu-tion by a community of one of its temporal problems; for both conceived that the divine will was mirrored in nature, which man could study by the use of his reason. This is the faith which has kept jurisprudence an honest and potent exercise through the ages, though the decline in religion has made it necessary to find other and secular names for its aims and technique.

A number of the British who thought that Joyce should have been acquitted had wholly lost this conception of the law. It seemed to them an interference with life, although life is what likes to make laws. They like to lay unfair stress on the inability of the courts to adapt themselves immediately to the age, which indeed is one of their characteristics. Politics and the law are always lagging behind the times, because the course taken by our existence is unpredictable, and it takes days and months and even years to present Parliament and the courts with knowledge of the eventualities they have to meet. Such people saw William Joyce as having smartly out-manoeuvred the law and as deserving of safety in recompense for having worsted that decrepit enemy. They even enjoyed the technical nature of his defence, which linked on to the delight that is often felt in people who have found a way through the law in grosser exercises than treason. Many people at the turn of the century were ready to cheer the cold shark Horatio Bottomley, because he had exploited the unforeseen situation created by the existence of a class which had a certain amount of investable capital and was ready to invest it without taking advice from a banker and stockbroker. It touched them neither in their hearts nor their sense of self-preservation that most of Bottomley's victims were people like themselves, whose savings were their only shield from actual

want in old age. Simply they derived pleasure from thinking of him as drinking three bottles of champagne a day
and keeping a racing stable on the proceeds of a form of
financial crime which the law then had not learned to
check. It opened to all of them the prospect that one day
they might find some such opportunity of gain, easier than
honesty and unpunishable, and that life would be proved
moral nonsense. Half a century later the emphasis was not
on wealth but on licence of conduct. Those who hankered
for a meaningless universe wanted Joyce to go free so that
they could see a man whose crime they knew by the testi-
mony of their own ears escape the law. Joyce himself would
have had none of this. As might be expected, he was not
with those who said that he was a vile man but should not
have been hanged. What might not have been expected
was that his attitude was the exact reverse. He maintained
that he was not a vile man, but thought England was right
in hanging him. He would have taken it as proof of our
national decadence that since the year he died no spies have
been sentenced to death.

CHAPTER 4

The life of William Joyce is worthwhile studying in detail because he represents a type of revolutionary who is for the moment obsolete, though it is possible, if the later models fail, that he may yet be found in currency again. He begins by being a touching figure. For there is no sight more touching than a boy who intends to conquer the world, though there is that within himself which means he is more likely to be its slave. Young William Joyce was such a boy, and took the first step to conquest all right, for he was brave. Perhaps he really lay deep in the heather so that he might tell the Black and Tans whether the three men they were looking for were still in the farmhouse in the fold of the hills; perhaps he only pressed on the Black and Tans information that was of no service to them. But he did go through the forms of attachment to a dangerous cause because he was ready to die if death was nobler than life. That he was mistaken in his estimate of where nobility lay is not a great count against him, since he was only fifteen. And behind his political folly was a grain of wisdom. He liked the scarlet coats of the English garrisons, but it was

Mozart himself who asked in a letter if there was anything in life finer than a good scarlet coat, and all scarlet coats take up a common argument. They dissent from the dark earth and the grey sky, they insist that the bodies that wear them are upright, they are for discipline, either of drill or the minuet. It was not to be held against the boy that he preferred the straight-backed aliens in scarlet coats to his compatriots who slouched with hats crushed down on cowlicks and collars turned up round unshaven jaws, as they went about their performance of menial toil or inglorious assassination. His family—and he was loyal to his own blood—cultivated that preference. That the smart soldiers created the slouching assassins he could hardly have been expected to work out for himself at that age.

He came to London before his family; and his destiny sent him down to South London, and there was significance in that. South London is not the London where England can be conquered. It is not London at all, even calling itself by a vague and elided locution. 'Where do you live?' 'South the river.' The people on the other bank never speak of their landscape as 'north the river'. They may go down east, or up west, but they move within London, where the Houses of Parliament are, and the Abbey, and Buckingham Palace, and Trafalgar Square, and the Law Courts, and St Paul's and the Mansion House, and the Bank and the Mint, and the Tower and the Docks. The house where William Joyce first took up his dwelling on the other side of the Thames stood in one of those streets which cover the hills round Clapham Junction like a shabby striped grey counterpane. It was a tiny little house, and he was there only as a lodger while he got the formalities arranged for his studies at Battersea Polytechnic. It was from there that he sent in the completed enrolment form to the University of London Committee for Military Education, thus taking what he believed to be his first step toward the conquest of England. It was going to be of no consequence at all that he and his family had had to leave Ireland. He would conquer the larger island instead.

When his father came south in the following year, he became, with superb adaptability, a grocer; and he took the step, unlooked-for in a dazed immigrant, of establishing his family in a house as delightfully situated as any in London. Allison Grove is a short road of small houses which has been hacked out from the corner of the gardens of a white Regency villa in the greenest part of Dulwich, a queer cheap insertion in a line of stately properties. It has its own great sycamore tree and many syringas, and the most agreeable surroundings. Not far off is Mill Pond, still a clear mirror of leaves and sky, and beyond it Dulwich College amidst its groves and playing-fields. To the south a golf-course makes a wide circle of mock country, bound by suburbs rising on round hills. To the north, behind the line of mansions into which Allison Grove intrudes, lies the handsome Victorian formality of Dulwich Park, with its winding carriage drives and its large sheet of ornamental water. An Irish family that had to come to London could not have more cleverly found a part of London more spaciously and agreeably unlike itself, and their house was cleverly found too. One side of Allison Grove had been built in Victorian times; the harsh red brick had been piled up in shapes as graceless as outhouses and to heights obviously inconvenient for the housewife. But the houses were amply planned for their price, and one of them gave room enough for the Joyce parents and William and his two younger brothers and his little sister.

The neighbours who thought the Joyces outlandish but likeable, though curiously arrogant, all noted that William was the apple of the family's eye, and they could understand it, for the boy had an air of exceptional spirit and promise. But during the day at Battersea Polytechnic he must have suffered many defeats, being tiny, alien, and ineradicably odd. In 1923 he was to experience what was to his inordinate pride, the pride of a very small man, the crushing defeat of failure in two subjects in his Intermediate Science examination.

His reaction was characteristic. There was nothing disgraceful in his failure. He was only seventeen; his schooling had been much interrupted, first by his disposition to argue with his Jesuit teachers, since as the son of a Catholic father and a Protestant mother he never accepted Roman Catholicism easily. Later he was distracted from his books by civil war and change of country. He could have tried again. But on this failure he immediately abandoned his intention of becoming a Bachelor of Science and turned his back on Battersea Polytechnic. It is to be noted that more depended on his failure or success than he can have expected when he was a child. With exile his father Michael Joyce had entered on a declining scale of prosperity. He had come back from America thirteen years before with a substantial capital sum; he was to grow poorer and poorer, and when he died in 1941 he left only six hundred and fifty pounds. He himself attributed his impoverishment to the failure of the British Government to compensate him adequately for the burning of his house and the destruction of other property of his at the hands of the Sinn Feiners. This complaint was, in the opinion of a detached observer with some knowledge of practical affairs, well founded. William Joyce must have felt he could not afford to waste time. It is interesting to speculate just what effect this step had on his destiny. His ambition was very strong; and it just might have happened that if he had become a Bachelor of Science he would have recognized the easy and brilliant future which this age offers to the Communist scientist.

As it was, he went to the Birkbeck College for Working Men, which is a part of the University of London, a physically sombre though intellectually vigorous institution, hidden in the dark streets between Holborn and the Law Courts, and there he studied the English language and literature and history. He made an excellent though odd student and passed with first-class honours, though for the first two years of his course he was subject to a new distracting influence. In 1923 he joined the British Fascists. This was an odd instance of his inability to get the hang of the world he meant to conquer. Mussolini had come to power in 1922, and warm admiration was felt for him by numerous persons of influence in England; and a young man might well have sincerely shared that mistaken admiration and at the same time have wished to use that admiration as a means of personal advancement. But joining the British Fascists was not the way to make that advance. This body was never numerous and had few links with the influential admirers of Mussolini, having been promoted by an elderly lady, member of a military family, who was overcome by panic when she read in the newspaper that the British Labour party was sending a delegation to an International Conference in Hamburg. Her creation was patronized by a certain number of retired Army men and a back-bench M.P. and an obscure peer or two; but the great world mocked at it, and it had as aim the organization of amateur resistance to any revolution that might arise. It was a charade representing the word 'barricade'.

If William Joyce wanted either to hold a commission in the Regular Army, or to teach, or to become a journalist, membership in this universally unfavoured movement was certain to be prejudicial to his hopes. It may be said that he was still young, but many a boy and girl of seventeen, determined to rise in the world, has cast a canny eye on such strategical pitfalls. He, however, had from first to last none of the adaptability normally given by ambition. But there were more positive factors than mere obtuseness at work here. The party, as well as holding meetings of its own, made a practice of interrupting and breaking up the Communist meetings which were being held in London, especially in the East End, often with the aim of explaining and defending Bolshevik Russia. Joyce, according to a tutor who coached him at this time, took these affrays with extreme seriousness. He spoke of the Communists with real horror: as, in fact, Orangemen would speak of Sinn Feiners. There was working in him a nostalgia for the Irish situation. Later, in the air raids, we were all to learn that danger is a better stimulant than champagne until the fatigue is too great. William Joyce had experienced that gaiety when he was too young to know real fatigue. Hence he enjoyed, with a constant driving esurience, street fighting.

No sport could be meaner. The thin boy wearing spectacles is cut off from his friends, he is hustled into an alley, his arms are twisted, his teeth are knocked in. But the sport was recommended to William Joyce by the memory of his courage in its springtime, and excessive deaths in Russia gave him his excuse. He was led into temptation.

In 1925 he left the British Fascists. This may have been because he became involved in certain internal dissensions which appeared, inevitably enough, in the movement; dog of a certain sort is always eating dog. Or it may have been because he feared to fail in his arts course as he had failed in his science course, and sacrificed his hobbies. But before long he had another and more urgent distraction.

A week after his twenty-first birthday, on 30 April 1927, he married a girl of his own age, a chemist's assistant, the daughter of a dentist, who was remarkable for her pleasant good looks. Because she was a Protestant, he, the son of an Irish Roman Catholic father, a pupil of the Jesuits, married her at the Chelsea Registry Office. He set up house in that district, and started on a phase of his life which gave him and his family a great deal of satisfaction. After he had taken his degree, with first-class honours, he continued in his studies in a post-graduate course in philology and later began a course in psychology at King's College. He had no difficulty in paying his way, for he had already, as a student, joined the staff of a tutorial college and was regarded as one of their best students. He had a real passion for teaching. He had a trick, another teacher remembered, of getting command of the minds of pupils who could not get going by teaching them chess.

It must be remarked that all these achievements brought him not an inch nearer any position of real power. He could never by any chance have been invited to join the staff of any school or college of conventional type, because of this curious atmosphere of illiteracy which hung about him. Only uneducated people accepted easily that he was learned. Educated people were always astounded to hear that he had been at a university. Even his handwriting, which was spiky and uneasy, suggested that he rarely took up his pen. Though he then went to work for the Conservative party, not only speaking for them but learning the technique of organization, and showing aptitude for both activities, it got him nowhere. He was not acceptable, in a deep sense. A police officer who had known William Joyce for many years, and had liked him, said hesitantly, for he was speaking a few days before the execution, that sometimes Joyce had reminded him, even in the days before the war, of a real criminal, of the sort that makes lags. It was not that he had then committed any crime, but because he, like the lags, 'did not seem to fit in anywhere'.

Between 1930 and 1933 his enthusiasm for the Conservative party flagged, and during this time he renewed his connexions with British Fascism, which had now much more to offer him and his special case. A number of obscure people in London were at that time conscious that a disaster was overhanging Europe. Those who foresee the future and recognize it as tragic are often seized by a madness which forces them to commit the very acts which make it certain that what they dread shall happen. So it was natural that some of these should join with the young men who were gratifying a taste for street fighting under the plea that they stood for order and Fascism, while others joined with the young men who were gratifying a taste for street fighting under the plea that they stood for order and Communism. Both were undermining the civilization which gave them power to pursue these curious pleasures. In this way, the Fascists and Communists had destroyed order and enabled Mussolini to seize power, and the same process was then taking place in Germany.

In Great Britain a Fascist Movement of some apparent substance had been formed by Sir Oswald Mosley, who was inspired by that impatience with evil which often produces evil. In 1931 he appeared at a by-election at Ashton-under-Lyne to support the candidature of a member of his New party, which was to be a Socialist party more drastic and dashing than the Labour party. His supporter was standing against a Conservative and an orthodox Labour candidate. When the results were announced at the town hall on election night he looked down at a sea of jeering faces who were exulting at this defeat for several reasons. Some were guffawing because a rich baronet should profess Socialism and because a man who was brilliant and handsome had suffered disappointment and humiliation; others because such a man had split the orthodox Labour vote and let in the Conservative. So Mosley said to a friend, 'These are the people who have got in the way of everybody who has tried to do anything since the last war.' It was a sensible enough observation; but making it, Mosley in his pride violated the just pride of others. He abandoned the attempt to wrestle with the vulgarity of the vulgar by argument and by example and decided to court them in their own fashion. Thereafter his agitation might have deceived the vulgar into crediting himself with a like vulgarity, and it looked as if he might seize power through their support.

Joyce was therefore valuable to Mosley just for those qualities which would have prevented his becoming an Army officer or a don. So the Fascist movement was ready to give him a place in a hierarchy, with which there went acclamation, a certain amount of money, travel abroad, and company which was of a certain distinction. The movement was not in all respects as Joyce would have had it. Though it happened to be led by Sir Oswald Mosley, he was in fact its follower rather than its leader. It had sprung up because people who, living in an established order, had no terror of disorder, had read too much in the newspapers about Mussolini and Hitler, and thought it would be exciting to create disorder on the same lines. If it had not arisen spontaneously it would have been fomented by foreign agents. It was a dynamic movement with roots that went deep and wide, and it did not impinge at any point on the world inhabited by the existing executive class. With the people that controlled politics, or commerce, or the professions, it had nothing to do. It grew beside them, formidable in its desire to displace them from that control, but separated from all contact with them as if a vast plate-glass window was between them. To no movement could the isolated William Joyce more appropriately have belonged.

It was Sir Oswald Mosley's peculiar function to give false hope to the British Fascists, to seem to lead them out of limbo and introduce them into the magnetic field of national power. Ill-informed about all conspicuous persons, they did not know that he was an outsider; he also had been born outside and not inside his environment. He had been born into the old governing class of the Tory aristocracy, but had brought his own plate-glass window into the world with him; and he had penetrated into the new governing class of the Labour party to the extent of holding office in the first Labour Government, but had formed no tie of liking or trust which would prevent it from preferring any other of its members to him. It is probable that William Joyce, with his incapacity for drawing any social inference whatsoever, was as blind as the rank and file to the qualities of failure inherent in Sir Oswald.

Within two years after Sir Oswald had founded the British Union of Fascists, William Joyce became his Director of Propaganda and Deputy Leader of his party. He lived then in a home which, though cheap and unfashionable, possessed its picturesque distinction. He was staying in a flat in a road clinging to the lip of an escarpment in the strangest spot in the strangeness of South London. It was far south of the river, where the tameness of town overspreads hills which, though insignificant in height, are wild in contour; and if it covers them with the tame shapes of houses it has to stack them in wild steepness. But above this suburban precipice the buildings themselves were wild with the wildness sometimes found in Victorian architecture. Outside the windows of his flat in Farquhar Road, two towers ran up into the sky and between them the torso of the Crystal Palace was at one and the same time a greenhouse and a Broad Church cathedral. In summer-time the night behind this didactic architectural fairy tale was often sprayed with the gold and silver jewels of Messrs Brock's fireworks, while a murmur of oh's and ah's and cheers rose from the crowds that walked in the gardens among the cement prehistoric animals which had been placed there in the mid-nineteenth century as illustrations to some thesis regarding the inevitability of progress and the usefulness of knowledge. A little way up the road was the Crystal Palace railway station, the most fantastic in London, so allusive, particularly in its cast-iron ornamental work, to uplifting Victorian festivity that it would not be surprising to find its platforms thronged by a choir singing an oratorio by Parry or Stainer. The windows on the other side of the house where Joyce lived looked down on the whole of London, across the Thames, over the imperial city, up to the green hills of Hampstead and Highgate. Tufts of tree-tops and a lack of roofs told where there were public parks; Joyce would point them out and say he had spoken in all of them. At night the lights of London make a spectacular theatre, and it is said that keen eyes can distinguish the light which burns above Big Ben to show that the House is still sitting. It was from this flat, on 4 July 1933, that William Joyce addressed the application for a passport which cost him his life. He desired it for the purpose of travelling to France and Germany.

It was a consciously illegal act, as he was not British. Or was it not quite that? The statement he made after his arrest makes it appear that he had never been sure about his nationality—which is to say, that he never made sure about it, that he never paid the visit to a solicitor which would have told him everything. He took a gamble on it. He took yet another gamble on standing for the two-seat constituency of Shoreditch as a Fascist candidate in the municipal elections of 1937. But success was far away; 2,564 people voted for him and 2,492 voted for another Fascist out of a total poll of 34,128.

He took another gamble when he gave rein to his passion for street fighting in his new post and in cold deliberation and with burning appetite applied himself to the technical problems of creating disorders; for a conviction might mean deportation, if he were discovered. It was about this time that Michael Joyce, who had long been reconciled to his beloved first-born, tore up his American passport and all documents relating to his American citizenship before the round, astonished eyes of his son Quentin, muttering his secret and commanding that it should be kept a secret, clairvoyant in his perception of the existence of the awful danger threatening his blood, but wrong, as clairvoyance nearly always is, concerning its precise nature and the point in time and space where that danger waited. He thought it was to be a common exile of his family across the sea, and must have seen it near at hand, about eighteen months after William Joyce took his first post with Mosley, when he and his chief, together with two local Fascists appeared at Lewes Assizes on a charge of riotous assembly at Worthing. They were acquitted after a trial that lasted for two days.

The incident at Worthing had followed a rhythm by which the normal course of life in provincial towns of England, and even in London itself, had been disturbed again and again during the past few years. First the local Fascists would announce well in advance that Sir Oswald Mosley was coming to hold a meeting in the largest local hall. Truculent advertisements and parades would prevent the town from forgetting it. The idea of violence would suddenly be present in the town. The proper course for those who were anti-Fascist was to abstain from all action on the day of the meeting, to stay in their houses and ignore it; but the idea of violence would enter into them also, and they would feel under a compulsion to attend the meetings and interrupt and provoke the stewards to throw them out. Then relatives and friends would know what they were thinking, and grow tense with dread. On the day of the meeting Sir Oswald Mosley and his party would arrive in a town already in the grip of hysteria, and there would come with them sinister paraphernalia; a complete counterfeit of all necessary preparations for the battle which could be regarded as defensive. There were men in uniform carrying weapons, truncheons made of shot-loaded sections of hose-pipe sealed with lead, armoured cars; ambulances complete with doctors and nurses—making a picture that meant danger, that aroused fear, that provoked the aggression which is fear's defence. The anti-Fascists, who had at first expelled the idea of violence from their minds and then reluctantly readmitted it, gathered, unstrung by this abhorred mental guest, round the hall in which the Fascist intruders were holding their meeting, spinning out words to cover the emptiness of a programme that contained nothing but antisemitism and an intention to establish dictatorship against the general will. When the Fascists came out they paraded in front of the crowd, bearing themselves inso-lently, until they provoked hostile demonstrations. Having provoked these, they assaulted the demonstrators, who struck back. So the civil order which generation after gen-eration of Englishmen had insisted on creating, in despite of tyranny and the lawlessness of their own flesh, lay dead in the street.

At Lewes this foolish and horrible story was told once more. The meeting had been over at ten. A hostile but inactive crowd had been waiting outside the hall. Mosley's lieutenants came into the street, bearing themselves in the jack-booted way, with elbows bent and clenched fists swinging. They began to speak in offensive tones to the people standing by. One paused in front of a boy of seventeen, a post-office messenger, and said something to him. The boy did not answer, and the Fascist asked, 'Don't you understand English?' The boy, looking at the Fascist's black shirt, said 'I don't understand Italian', and the Fascist hit him. At Lewes Assizes, Sir Patrick Hastings, while cross-examining this boy, asked him, 'Can you think of anything more insulting than what you did say?' It is of course a barrister's duty to get his client out of the dock, and Sir Patrick was defending the four Fascists; and he had the right to ask any question he thought proper. But it is interesting to remember that Mosley had visited Fascist Rome not long before and had taken the salute with Mussolini at a review.

Sir Patrick was no doubt encouraged by the atmosphere of the court. There were sound reasons why this should not be wholly unfavourable to the defendants. It was obvious that the Fascists could not be regarded as solely responsible for the riot. That the anti-Fascists had sinned as well as being sinned against was shown by the number of tomatoes they had thrown at Mosley and his lieutenants; these could hardly have been found lying to hand in the streets of Worthing at ten o'clock at night. And, truth to tell, some of the anti-Mosley pamphlets sold in the street certainly contained a great deal of nonsense. They implied that Mosley had promised Malta to Mussolini and parts of the British Empire to Hitler, and, as it would have been impossible for either dictator to give Mosley effective help to seize power in England, and as once he was the dictator of England he would have been their superior in resources, it is hard to see why he should have made any such commitment. Moreover, he appeared to have a genuine passion for the British Empire. It is possible that some of the anti-Fascist organizations were providing an opposition hardly less irresponsible and professional and dangerously itinerant than the Fascists.

During the trial the judge made certain interventions. A witness for the prosecution affirmed, when questioned about an incident in a certain street, that 'the whole affair seemed to be a joke on the part of the crowd'. This statement made Mr Justice Branson request: 'Tell us one of the jokes. I am always interested in good jokes.' The witness replied, 'They were singing "Mosley's got the wind up" and that sort of thing.' Mr Justice Branson majestically inquired, 'Do you call that a joke?' He also had passages with the police witnesses. It appeared that a local Fascist and his wife, who lived in Worthing, had sent several passionately apprehensive telephone messages to the police-station before and during the meeting. One was sent from the hall where the meeting was being held. 'Tell Superintendent B— to send some men down to restore order. If it is not done I shall go out and take the law into my own hands.' The constable who received this message took no action, because his superior officers were already on the spot outside the meeting. Mr Justice

Branson commented severely on his failure to act. Later a sergeant was examined who gave a picture of the debauch of savagery with which the police force of this seaside town had had to deal that night. In a typical passage a witness described how he had seen Fascists rush to the doorway of a chemist's shop, had followed them and when they had run away had found a person lying on the pavement unconscious, and then had turned round and seen another person, who was one of the witnesses in the trial, lying in the road, also unconscious. Mr Justice Branson interrupted this witness to say: 'I understood you to use the phrase, "The crowd which first chased down South Street." Was there a crowd which chased down South Street?' The Sergeant answered, 'There was a large number of people.' Mr Justice Branson asked, 'Why do you change your language? One expects in these cases that police will give their evidence fairly and frankly. Just bear that in mind in answering the rest of the questions.'

It was not surprising that William Joyce was acquitted at Lewes. There was no evidence to connect him with the riot that had taken place, and it was said by Sir Patrick Hastings that his name did not appear in any of the depositions. The other three defendants were also acquitted. At the close of the case for the prosecution the judge said he must take the responsibility of telling the jury that it should find a verdict of not guilty. As the jury expressed its full concurrence with his direction, and announced that it had been its intention to request that the evidence for the defence should not be heard, since the prosecution had failed to make out its case, and as the cases of assault which had been brought against some of the defendants in the local courts had been dismissed, the effect of the trial on William Joyce must have been intoxicating. Nevertheless, the Lewes trial may well have exercised a powerful influence on William Joyce's determination to travel the road that led to the gallows.

Indeed, the courts of law, civil as well as criminal, provided considerable encouragement for any ambitious Fascist at that time. But in the civil courts it was hardly the lawyers who could be held responsible. Virtue has its peculiar temptations, particularly when it is practised as a profession. The good are so well acquainted with the evil intentions of those whom they consider to be wicked that they sometimes write as if the wicked candidly express their intentions instead of, as is customary, veiling them in decent dissimulations. This has on many occasions led to the award of heavy damages against the good in cases brought under the laws of libel and slander by the wicked. The anti-Fascist Press were not mindful enough of this danger when they dealt with Mosley, whom they considered to be wicked. In one libel action Sir Oswald Mosley won, and rightly won, a verdict entitling him to five thousand pounds damages, and his costs. It must have seemed to William Joyce that society had gone a long way towards certifying that Fascism was not incompatible with its institutions, and it must have seemed to him that the opposition was unscrupulous and anti-social.

The daily routine of his work must have encouraged him in this delusion that he and his kind enjoyed the acquiescence, even the fondness, of society. It was unfortunate that the police liked him. They did not show him this favour because they shared his faith. It is a mistake to think that the police favoured the Fascists over the Communists—as they certainly did—on political grounds. There were, of course, policemen, as there were generals and admirals, who were deceived by the Fascist's use of the Union Jack and slogans about Britain into thinking them conservative patriots instead of international revolutionaries. There were others who regarded the Communists as blood-stained Bolsheviks, and admired the Fascists as their enemies. But there were many who thought, and both common sense and wisdom was with them, that if the Communists had ignored the Fascist meetings and refrained from interrupting them, the Fascists would have been checkmated, since they would not then have been able to exercise violence and plead that they were defending the right of free speech. They would then have had to attack Communist meetings or make unprovoked assaults on Jews in order to get their street fighting; and in that case policemen who arrested Fascists would have been able to get them convicted. As it was, they were constantly forced by the Communists' action into arresting Fascists who were discharged by magistrates because they pleaded that they acted under provocation; and there is nothing a policeman likes less than seeing the charge against a man he has arrested being dismissed. This is partly, though not entirely, a matter of pride. It also concerns his promotion. If there is any blame to be attached to the men involved in these proceedings, it should not fall on the police but on the magistrates, who were so very often satisfied that the Fascists had been provoked. But, for magistrates and police alike, the situation was exasperating. If a man went to a meeting held by a party which advertised its loyalty to king and country through every material and spiritual loudspeaker, and which was notorious for its easy resort to violence, and he remained seated during the singing of the National Anthem, police and magistrates alike felt a disinclination to concern themselves with what subsequently befell him. They were, of course, wrong. Their business was to suppress violence, however it had been provoked. But such citizens, and all those who played the Fascist game by accepting their challenge, were either irritating masochists or troublemakers obeying Communist instruction.

If the police liked Joyce it was because he persuaded them he was alleviating this ugly situation. He was a fine disciplinarian. His men were truly his. On them he now could play all the tricks of charm that take in young hero-worshippers: the recollections of a previous encounter, stated with a suggestion that an ineffaceable impression had been made, a permanent liking engendered; the sternness broken by a sudden smile. He had also learned the trick of turning his puniness into an asset of terror: a little man can be terrible when he outstares a taller and stronger subordinate who has been insolent to him, and coldly orders another subordinate, still taller and stronger, to inflict a brutal punishment on him. 'Joyce really had his men under control,' said a member of the police force, 'and he was always fair to us. We could never come to an understanding with the Communists; if we saw the leaders it was hard to get on terms with them, and if we did persuade them to alter a plan they didn't seem able to make their men carry out the alteration. But if I went to Joyce and told him that his men were doing something that wasn't fair on the police, trying us too hard or interfering with our time off, he'd have his men right off that job in half an hour, and there'd be no grumbling. And he always kept his word, we found him very straight.'

This officer—and he spoke for many of his colleagues—thought Joyce a far abler man than Mosley. It is possible that William Joyce was, at that time, a person of real and potent charm offering the world what Blake said pleased it most, 'the lineaments of gratified desire'. He saw his path to greatness clear before him. He experienced the sharp joys of public speaking and street fighting nearly every night, and every month or so the more prolonged orgy of the great London or provincial meetings. Moreover, the routine of Fascism freshened and liberated the child in its followers. Mosley had taken a black old building in King's Road, Chelsea, formerly a Teachers' Training College, where he housed his private army of the whole-time members of the British Union of Fascists; and there life was a boy's dream. Uniforms were worn that were not really uniforms, that at once claimed and flouted authority, as adolescence does; there was discipline, savage (and therefore sadistically sweet) while it lasted, but perfectly eluctable, not clamped down on a definite period of time by the King's Regulations; corridors were patrolled by sentries beetling their brows at nothing, executive officers sat at desks laden with papers alluding to mischief as yet too unimportant to justify authority in taking steps to check it; dead-end kids who could call what was dead alive and the end the beginning, innocently and villainously filled rubber truncheons with lead. There is nothing like infantilism for keeping the eyes bright and the skin smooth.

At this time, too, Joyce must have been intoxicated by new experiences of several kinds. His family have denied that he ever went to Germany before 1939. But others believed that he made the journey more than once and shared in the long, sterile orgasm of the Nuremberg Rally, held on the great barren place which once had been rich farmland, where crowds, drunken with the great heat, entered into union with a man who was pure nihilism, who offered militarism and defeat, regulation and anarchy, power and ruin, the cancellation of all. That was a deep pleasure, surrounded by shallower ones; the drives through the entrancing country, scored with the great works which German Joyces had ordained by a wave of the hand, the visits to the fine villas which German Joyces had made their own and stuffed with works of art, the eating and drinking from the Gothic and Renaissance tables of German Joyces where the heavy goblets stood on Genoese velvet. He at least heard of such joys, and in his own country he frequented the homes of the wealthy Mosleyite supporters, though he perhaps knew there less than the absolute enjoyment Germany could have given or did give him.

Few of the upper-class supporters of Mosley were intellectually distinguished in any way that induced the relinquishment of social prejudice. Only an eccentric, equally distinguished as a physicist and a steeplechaser, and a peer whose enthusiasm for Fascism was part of his passion for the grotesque and wholly conditional upon its failure to realize its objects, come to mind as probably unbiased by class feeling in their response to charm; and of what they would have considered charm William Joyce had none. Of course he had his wit; everybody who met him in England or Germany agrees that he never talked for long without putting a twist on a sentence that surprised the hearer into laughter. He had also the same pleasantness that was remarked on so often by the officials who had charge of him during his last days. But he was not, as they say, a gentleman. The other upper-class supporters of Mosley were for the most part professional soldiers and sailors, usually in their fifties; and of these some asked William Joyce to their houses out of a sense that they should recognize his services to the movement. He was to them, nevertheless, like an officer risen from the ranks. Awkwardness occurred. One week-end he was a guest at the country house of an army man who kept a large stable; and on Sunday morning the host let his guests try some of his less valuable horses. William Joyce, who had learned to ride as a boy in Mayo and Galway, handled his horse so well that he was allowed to try another one, a fine and difficult thoroughbred. The host's father, an old gentleman so deaf that he could not tell whether he was shouting or whispering, stood among the other guests and watched. 'How marvellously Mr Joyce rides', a lady bawled into his ear. 'Yes!' he bawled back. 'But not like a gentleman.' Nobody was sure whether Mr Joyce had heard.

When a man's social horizon widens, his sexual horizon rarely stays where it was. There was a rackety recruit to Fascism, a wealthy young man who had suffered the initial handicap of being expelled from an ancient school, not for any perversity but for precocity induced by the enterprise of an American actress, who took a cottage near the school for the summer term. He invited Joyce to a shooting-party, where he met the sister of an Irish peer and was profoundly impressed by her. She felt no corresponding emotion and probably never knew of his. It may have been such disturbing encounters which first suggested to William Joyce what might not have occurred to him if he had stayed where he was born, that he need not always stay married to the same woman. From the beginning, it is said, his life with the girl he had married when they were both twenty-one had been a cycle of romantic ecstasy and quarrels and impassioned reconciliations; he would turn anything into a fight. He took it for granted, too, that he should spend an amount of time with men friends, which must have made home life exiguous. During his time of service with Mosley his relations with his wife grew more and more purely quarrelsome, and in 1936, although they had by then two little daughters, this marriage was dissolved.

At a Fascist rally in Dumfries, William Joyce met the woman who was to become his second wife, a pretty and spirited girl from Lancashire, which had been Joyce's second home as a boy. She was the daughter of a textile warehouse manager and an enthusiastic member of the B.U.F., a secretary and a trained dancer who often performed at cabaret shows given at festive gatherings of North Country Fascists. She was slender and graceful and took her dancing seriously, but she gladly threw away her ambitions to serve her husband and his ambitions. Though outsiders thought that Joyce's second marriage followed the same pattern of ecstasy and dissension and reconciliation as his first, there was apparently a deep and true love between him and his wife which was to endure to his death. There is indeed to be recognized in the conventional prettiness of her face a certain not conventional solemnity and submissiveness, as if she knew she should bow to a great force when it visited her; and it appears certain that she believed William Joyce to be that great force.

He left South London, which had been his home since he was a boy with the exception of a few brief periods; which was still the home of his father, Michael Joyce, and his mother, Queenie, and his brothers and sister; which was his appropriate home. Where the drab rows of little houses and the complacent villas shamed their builders by losing their drabness and their mediocrity because of the hills on which they were set, there he should have gone on living, this puny and undistinguished little man who was wild with a desire for glory. He moved to the north side of the river, but not to imperial London. When he married his second wife he was living in one of the dreariest spots in the dreariness east of Brompton Cemetery: a place where the cats limp and have mange, and the leaves bud brown in the spring. It was the first of his London homes which was characterless. He might have chosen it when he had ceased to care whether the routine of life was pleasant because he was so preoccupied with the crisis of the future.

CHAPTER 5

Shortly after his marriage William Joyce began to contemplate deserting Mosley and becoming an agent of Nazi
Germany. He did not get on well with his leader. It can be
taken as certain that, if the police thought him more able
than Mosley, he held the same opinion with some intensity.
Moreover, it is impossible that Joyce was blind to the gulf
that yawned between one part of the Fascist Movement
and another. The wife of one of the few Fascist leaders who
were in the inner ring with Mosley was asked, 'Did you and
your husband ever ask Joyce to your house?' She answered
in horror, 'Oh, no, never. That was the great thing that
worried us all, about what we were to do after Tom [as
Mosley was known to his familiars] had become dictator.
We didn't know how we were going to get rid of all those
dreadful common people we had had to use to get power.'
It is unlikely that the sentiments behind the remarks would
have remained hidden from the cold eyes of William Joyce,
and that he would have missed the political implication
behind them; and he may have asked himself just why
Mosley had chosen him as Deputy Leader of the party. It

would have seemed more natural that the position should be filled by one of the army or naval high-ranking officers who supported the movement, rather than by an insignificant little man with no social influence, for whom Mosley had no personal liking. William Joyce was tough enough to put the question in that form, and shrewd enough to answer it by admitting that his charm for Mosley was the obvious unlikelihood that he would set up as a rival for leadership of the movement.

There was also a difference between their outlook on policy, which became more marked as time went on, and in which the advantage lay with Joyce so far as simplicity was concerned. Mosley had started his movement before Hitler came to power; Mussolini had been his inspiration. But very shortly after 1933 the emotional interest of the British Fascist movement shifted to Germany. This was in every sense natural, for what makes every Fascist and Communist movement go round is the pickings for the boys; and the boys in Italy had never had anything like the swollen and novel pickings that came to the boys in Germany. Mosley seems, like many people, to have believed that Hitler was a man of supreme ability, and perhaps felt some personal liking for him. That he married his second wife in Hitler's presence may have signified either real affection for Hitler or a desire to build up an alliance by intimacy. William Joyce on his side venerated Hitler as he had never been able to venerate Mosley. While William Joyce was cold but naive, Mosley was hot-headed but sophisticated; he could argue with his own passions in defence, not of the truth, but of his own ends. Hence Mosley could bear to proclaim the Nazi doctrine of a totalitarian and anti-Semitic state without overt propaganda for Hitler. His line was to admit admiration for Hitler and Mussolini, but to deprecate any excessive interest in continental affairs and profess belief in isolationism. 'Mind Britain's Business' was his slogan; and he assured the public that if Hitler were given a free hand in Europe and were returned his mandated colonies, while we at home suppressed the Jews, the peace of the world would be guaranteed, and the British Empire would be immune from attack. But he was careful to say that if Hitler should ever attack the British Empire, its people would, of course, defend themselves, and would be victorious. William Joyce wanted to preach acclamation of Hitler as the saviour of the world on such unconditional terms that by implication it must be the duty of every good Briton to resist any British Government which took up arms against him.

Both these policies would work out to the same result. If Great Britain had pursued an isolationist policy and let Hitler conquer Europe, as Mosley wished, he would have had no reason to refrain from crossing the Channel and setting up what government he pleased; and there the matter would have remained, for it would have been extremely difficult for America to come to the aid of an invaded Great Britain which had acquiesced in the invasion of all the rest of Europe. In these circumstances it would certainly have been the Fascists from whom Hitler would draw his Quisling government. On the other hand, if the Fascists had devoted their energies in peacetime to the proclamation of the greatness of Hitler, as Joyce wished, and preached collaboration freely and frankly up to the declaration of the war (within the limits set down in the law of treason), then again it would seem the Fascists would furnish the Quislings when they were needed. Of the two policies, the one framed by Joyce frankly admitted the international character of Fascism, which makes a man ready to be a traitor to his country, his county, his town, his street, his family, himself, and loses its dynamic power if it does not act by and through this readiness for treachery. This was quite outside the framework of Mosleyism.

But policy was not the only subject of disagreement between Mosley and Joyce at this moment. Joyce was, for the first time in his life, troubled about money. He had been brought up in a household where there had always been enough to maintain the simple satisfaction of all needs. He had supported himself and his wife adequately on his earnings as a tutor, which he had been able to stretch by taking on extra classes. For his chief pleasures, which were public speaking and street fighting, he did not pay but was paid. For his lesser pleasures he could afford to pay. For example, he had a fine radiogram and a large library of records, chiefly operatic. Now, however, he had to make a home for himself and his second wife and support his first wife's children, and Mosley was paying him a small and inelastic salary. He needed an increase in pay just at the very time Mosley was least likely to give it. Mosley must have been in genuine financial difficulties. It is said that he was spending nine tenths of his income on the cause, but that went nowhere in maintaining a private army of anything from twelve hundred to two thousand, together with a great number of subsidized hangers-on. It is true that he was financed by some industrialists, and by some City firms, even including one or two who by reason of their origin should have been most careful not to compromise themselves in this direction. But these industrialists were not the great magnates who were persistently rumoured to be contributing to Mosley's funds; they were for the most part old gentlemen at the head of minor firms with only moderate means at their disposal. If ever the bigger City firms were sometimes more generous they were also more canny, and both alike were beginning to be less forthcoming. They had contributed because they had believed Mosley to be a stabilizing force in society. But do what he could, he could not prevent his movement from looking what it was, revolutionary. The increasing brutality of the brawls with Jews and Communists was betraying the nature of its inspiration.

Also, time was to reveal that the right sort of recruits were not coming in. There was only the odd distinguished man coming in now and then, such as Sir Arnold Wilson, an extremely able colonial administrator. Another writer of some standing and much charm supported the party, but it was too generally recognized that he had not been sober for thirty years for his political opinions to carry much weight. There should have been some appeal to the Kipling tradition in an officer who was the author of a bestseller about army life in the East, but he was unnegotiable by reason of his devotion to Oriental mysticism in its quainter manifestations. About this time a Fascist leader was driving a banker whom he regarded as a possible convert back from a week-end which had seemed very profitably spent, when he realized that they were passing the home of this officer author and suggested that they should stop and call on him. The banker was delighted. But the butler repelled them. The major was in, and the butler would take a message to him, but he could not possibly be seen. The Fascist persisted and finally the butler, who was a traditional butler, for this was a traditional home, broke down and said, 'It's no use, this is the day he spends sitting on the roof with his Yogi having his perpetual enema.'

British Fascism did hardly better with its aristocratic supporters. One of these bore a title founded by a historic personage of the first order. If anybody alluded in his hearing to his great ancestor 'the great Duke of —' his brows would contract and he would say huffily, 'The first Duke of —'. Later he was to give his life nobly in the war against Fascism, and this anecdote relates to a superficial oddity and not to the sum of him. It is worth while recalling only to explain the difficulties that Mosley was having in creating an impression of normality. Even with his numerous service members he had his difficulties. He had to handle these with care, lest possibly an officer of personal attractions and gifts for oratory and administration should dispute his leadership. But all the same, it was a pity that his most active service supporter should be stone-deaf, although it is true that deafness has more than once played a decisive part in our great island story; our pro-Bulgarian policy, which so disastrously endured for generations, was largely the work of a *Times* correspondent who travelled through the Balkans ceaselessly but without being able to hear a word that anyone said to him. Worst Mosleyite disappointment of all, however, was a wealthy and aristocratic young man, now dead, who created a most favourable impression at one of the Nuremberg Rallies, but was, like the friend named Guy

Burgess who accompanied him, a Communist deputed to infiltrate the Mosley Movement.

Naturally enough the movement was short of subscriptions, Joyce was paid no advance on salary commensurate with his services to the movement, and he was therefore left in a state of insecurity and with a feeling that Mosley had failed to fulfil the promise he had seemed to make to his obscure followers, the promise that those outside should find themselves at last inside, that the powerless should find themselves as equals among the powerful. Some time in the beginning of 1937, a police officer who knew Joyce found himself alone with him in a compartment in a late train from the Midlands which had a break-down. For a time they talked of impersonal matters, then, as the delay lengthened, fell into silence, which the police officer suddenly found himself breaking with the question, 'Joyce, what do you really think of Mosley?' He had no idea why he asked that question; he had heard nothing of any breach between the two. The little man, who had been huddled in fatigue, now fixed the police officer with eyes cold as ice. Joyce was famous among the British Fascists for his power to curse, and for the next ten minutes, quietly and steadily, he used it, then sank back into apparent slumber. The police officer paid him the classic compliment of saying that he never once repeated himself, and added that 'there was nothing ordinary in it', and he summed up its content as an opinion that 'Mosley was letting them down by doing his job so badly'. A few weeks later it was announced that Mosley had dismissed Joyce from his post as the Director of Propaganda and Deputy Leader of the party, for the reason that he was under a necessity to cut down on his salaried staff.

Within three weeks of leaving the B.U.F., Joyce had founded his British National Socialist League; and very soon afterwards he had an office in London and an official organ, *The Helmsman*. This was quick work; it also cost money. It is true that it did not cost much money, but then Joyce had almost none. He had gone back to his work as a tutor, and was doing well, but not so well that he could earn much more than would support himself and his wife and meet other obligations. The British National Socialist League could never boast a membership that was more than a fraction of the strength of the B.U.F., and never pretended to live on its subscriptions. The only subscriber to British National Socialist League funds who has been identified with any certainty was the old Scottish stockbroker whose sister was later to visit Joyce in prison, and he gave generously, but nothing that went into thousands. Joyce himself declared that he was financed by certain industrialists, but it seems most unlikely that any industrialist shrewd enough to have maintained his business would have thought it worth while to subsidize this lone little man who, however great his gift for organization, had now only a handful of followers to organize. There was, on the other hand, a great deal of German money lying about in England at that time, to be picked up by anybody who chose to take a certain amount of trouble.

How little that trouble needed to be, how that money could petition to be picked up, can be illustrated by the case of the two young women with strong right-wing views who thought it would be amusing to write and publish a news-letter. After a couple of numbers appeared they were approached by a man holding a teaching position in a certain university, who told them that he would finance their news-letter to the extent of two or three thousand pounds, provided only that they published a certain amount of approving references to Hitler. If William Joyce accepted money from such sources, he was breaking no law. In the United States it is a crime to take money from the representative of a foreign power without registering as a foreign agent, but in England such an act is lawful and it would be easy to name a number of English persons on the Right and the Left who have benefited by transactions with continental governments anxious to have friends in England. The United States law is, however, rendered nugatory by the power of bribery to take forms other than cash payments. There, as in England, publishing houses specially founded for the purpose can commission propagandist works, and the management of societies for friendship toward specific countries offer well-paid jobs, while alien governments can buy whole editions of books or subscribe for thousands of issues of a journal. It is not impossible that Joyce accepted money, directly or indirectly, from those with whom he conspired, but it is quite certain that he did not commit treason for the sake of gain.

Some time after Joyce had left the British Union of Fascists and set up his own movement, he and his wife had moved to a very pleasant home, the most expensive home he occupied in his whole life: the top flat of a doctor's house in a soberly agreeable square in South Kensington. It would never have been let to him had he presented himself as the prospective tenant. But it was taken by Angus MacNab, whose obvious good breeding and gentleness impressed the doctor and his wife very favourably. He explained to them that he was setting up in business as a coach in partnership with a friend named William Joyce, and at a second interview brought with him Mrs Joyce, whom they thought not so well bred as he was, but pretty and agreeable. On these samples of the household they concluded the transaction, and were disconcerted when its third person arrived with the removal van, which contained a prodigious amount of books and some poor sticks of furniture, and proved to be a queer little Irish peasant who had gone to some pains to make the worst of himself. The wearing of uniforms by private persons was by then illegal; so he and MacNab always wore black sweaters of a shape calculated to recall the Fascist black shirt. His suit and trench-coat were in imitation of Hitler's turn-out and were deliberately kept dirty and shabby; he cropped his hair in the Prussian style and never wore a hat; he always carried a very thick stick; and he bore himself with a deliberate aggressiveness. The doctor and his wife instantly took a dislike to him, which they were to find not unjustified when they saw more of the household. They liked his wife and thought he treated her tyrannously, overworking her and giving her no thanks, in the peasant way. He was tiresomely exigent about his meals; and not only had she to cook them, but had to wash up afterwards, and then run off to help at the League office in the day-time, and in the evenings at meetings. But the doctor and his wife had to admit that she adored him and that he evidently made her very happy.

They had other complaints against him. Their new tenants were indubitably noisy. Joyce had always loved noise.

A young man who knew him during his first marriage tells how he learned chess from him in a tiny room just big enough to hold two chairs, a table, and a radiogram which blared continually at full blast. It was torture for the pupil; Joyce took it as natural. Here the household banged doors and stamped about when they came in excited from their meetings, and sometimes gave rowdy parties. To one of them they invited the doctor's wife, who happened to be alone that evening. She was not reassured. Some of the guests were wild Irishmen—the same that attended his trial. These were for the most part from families with the same roots as the Joyces, who had been supporters of the British occupation of Ireland and who had had to leave the country for safety's sake when Home Rule was granted. One among these was the son of a man who had performed an act of charity towards a man dying of gun-shot wounds beside the road without inquiring into his political affiliations, was consequently victimized by his neighbours till he was obliged to take refuge in England, and there died in poverty, leaving his family aggrieved because they had received no adequate compensation from the British Government. The doctor's wife was unaware of the pathetic antecedents of these merrymakers, but she was disconcerted by the vehement quality of the merriment they made, and she came to her own conclusions about a gentleman with long hair who was wearing a scarlet cloak and a pectoral cross, and who introduced himself as the monarch of an Eastern European nation. It was not revealed to her that he had once been sentenced to a term of imprisonment for the publication of obscene poetry, but she felt there was something a little odd about him.

Nevertheless, the doctor and his wife did not attempt to terminate the lease. They were moved to this forbearance partly by their kindly feeling towards Mrs Joyce, who, they foresaw, would suffer greatly in one way or another through her marriage. They also liked MacNab, who was amiable and fantastical. Once when Joyce had gone off with the key to the flat and a pipe had burst inside it, MacNab, explaining that he had been a leading member of the Oxford Alpine Club, swarmed up the back of the Kensington house, by pipes and window-ledges and gutters, till he found a window open on the fifth storey. But the doctor and his wife developed more serious reasons than these for tolerance. One of their sons was taken ill and had to miss a term or two at his boarding-school, and during this period MacNab and William Joyce coached him, the one in Greek and mathematics, the other in Latin and French. The parents found the boy was getting better teaching than he had ever had in his life, as they discovered that these two strange men really cared for the things of the mind, really possessed unusual intellectual capacity. After that they sometimes asked their tenants down to their sherry parties; and they found to their surprise that though William Joyce was so obviously odious in so many ways, so vulgar, so pushing, so lacking in sweetness, many of their guests found his conversation interesting and amusing and even charming. They were baffled. They did not know what they wanted to do about their odd lodger, and the doing of it might not have been easy. The rent of the flat was paid with perfect regularity. It would have been difficult to break the lease except on very contestable grounds, and contest was certainly not out of Joyce's line.

So it seemed as if this exile was to lose his rootlessness in a place that asked roots to grow, and promised the grown plant pleasantness. Joyce's flat looked down on a communal garden of the sort that makes South Kensington so pleasantly green; the houses which back on them have their dining rooms built out into this garden. In summer-time the ladies of these houses often sat with their friends among tubs of flowers on the flat roofs of these dining-rooms, taking tea and looking down on their well-schooled children, who played on the lawns below. In late summer-time, in the year 1938, William Joyce sat in his pleasant home and applied for the renewal of his passport. It might be assumed that he had been sent for by someone who wished him to go abroad. It might also be assumed that he had not expected this summons, for he had let his passport expire without applying for its renewal. It had run out on 6 July. This was 24 September: five days before the Munich Agreement was signed. Nothing is gained by the postponement of an application for the renewal of a passport. At whatever date the application is made, it is renewed from the date of its expiry. It is possible that William Joyce felt no exultation at all while he was filling in his application form. He had faced danger as a boy, but that was nearly twenty years ago. Ever since then he had lived cradled in the safety of the civil order of England which he and his Fascist friends and Communist enemies were vowed to destroy, and safety becomes a habit. He must have liked the green dignity of this garden part of Kensington; it was like the home of his boyhood, which was also in one of the green corners of London, down in Allison Grove. He must have liked the setting of his life, and also its core. He liked teaching and he had his meetings and he was still deeply and romantically in love with his wife. If he had given an undertaking to leave that home when a certain voice called him, then he must daily have known real distress.

That time Joyce was let off and the wind of danger blew and fell again; and immediately after Munich, Joyce lost a valuable colleague who withdrew into the shelter of a pacifist organization which he then started on his own. It was as if he had caught some intimations of the end to which Joyce's policy was to lead him, and recoiled. At that time, too, Joyce began to lose the friendship of his land-lords; and the German radio sounded too loud through the house, the hiccoughing piano achieved the Horst Wessel song too often. The breach widened when Hitler walked into Czechoslovakia; the doctor and his wife were standing in the hall aghast at the news when Joyce came in, and asked him, 'Now what do you think of Hitler?' Joyce said, without a smile, 'I think him a very fine fellow,' and went on his way up to his flat. MacNab came in a little later. The doctor and his wife pressed him for his opinion; and he, too, approved. The curious friendship between the two households, so unequal in social background and in char-acter, faded from that moment, though the doctor and his wife still showed kindliness to Mrs Joyce. Joyce, working alone, worked frantically. He spoke to every society that would let him inside its doors; in the warmer weather he had an open-air meeting every day, and sometimes several in one day. It was as if he were trying to leave an impres-sion on the public mind that could be counted upon to endure; and indeed he partially succeeded in this aim. An enormous number of people in the low-income groups heard him speak, some during the years when he was with Mosley, and even more during the period when he was his own master.

Many people in the higher-income groups had also their contact with Joyce, but they did not know it. Anybody who was advertised as a speaker at a meeting appealing for funds or humane treatment for refugees from Nazi persecution would receive by every post, for many days before the meeting, threatening messages, couched always in the same words, and those words always so vague that the writers of them could not have been touched by the law. They were apt to come by the last post, and the returning householder, switching on the light, would see them piled up on the hall table, splinters from a mass of stupidity that might not, after all, be finite and destructible, but infinite and conterminous with life. Their postmarks showed they came from Manchester, Bristol, Bournemouth, Bethnal Green, Glasgow, Colchester. All over the country there were those who wished that the stranger, being hungry, should not be fed, being naked should not be clothed. Goats and monkeys, as Othello said, goats and monkeys; and the still house would seem like a frail and besieged fortress. This device was the invention of William Joyce. The people who heard him in the streets sometimes saw this alliance with crime openly displayed. A number of his meetings were provocative of the violence he loved; he was twice tried for assault at London police courts during the year preceding the outbreak of war, though each time the wind that sat in so favourable a quarter for Fascists blew him out with an acquittal. But it is incontestable that he often used all his powers, his harsh, sneering, cajoling, denatured, desperate voice, his quick and twisting humour, his ability to hammer a point home on a crowd's mind, to persuade the men and women he saw before him of the advantages of dictatorship, the dangers of Jewish competition and high finance, the inefficiency of democracy, the greatness and goodness of Hitler, and his own seriousness. But these audiences were not much interested in his arguments and were shrewd enough in their judgement of him. Many remembered him seven years afterwards. Only a very few said, 'I liked him.' Most said, 'He had the most peculiar views, but he really was an extraordinary chap', or some such words. 'Extraordinary' was what they called him, nearly all of them. But this impression might not have served Joyce so ill had the days brought forth what he expected. If the Germans had brought him with them when they invaded England and had made him their spokesman, many Londoners might have listened to him with some confidence, because in a scene which conquest would have made terrifying in its unfamiliarity he was a familiar figure.

William Joyce seemed to hear a second summons from abroad eleven months after the first. During that time his circumstances changed. In July he had left his agreeable home in South Kensington, at his own instance. In June he had suddenly written to the doctor saying that, with much regret, he must confess himself unable to carry out his three years' lease, which had still another year to run; the number of his pupils had, he explained, suddenly showed a sharp decline. The doctor answered, possibly not without some feeling of relief, that Joyce was at full liberty to sub-let the flat, and this Joyce undertook to do. One day, before they left, the doctor's wife met Mrs Joyce on the stairs and, with the extreme sweetness and generosity this couple always showed their strange tenants, paused to tell her how sorry she was that their connexions must end for so sad a reason. She said, 'All our fortunes vary, you know. One goes up and one comes down and then one comes up again, so you mustn't worry if things are bad.' To her astonishment Mrs Joyce burst into tears, flung her arms round her neck, and sobbed out, 'You do not know how bad they are, you have no idea how bad they are.'

About this time Joyce was importuned by a strange visitor. A man who, like so many of the British National Socialist League, was Irish, rang the bell marked 'Joyce' that was beside the doctor's bell at the front door. Joyce came down, opened the door, looked at the visitor, slammed it, and went upstairs again. The visitor went on ringing, and began to pound on the knocker. MacNab came down, white-faced, and opening the door parleyed with the visitor, but, like Joyce, retreated. Out on the porch the visitor rang the bell and hammered on the door and began to shout. The doctor's manservant went out and tried to send him away; he cried out that he must see William Joyce, no one else would do. The door was shut, he remained outside, crying out in accusation, in imploration, in panic, as one who knew a great shame was to be committed and could not stop it. The police would have been fetched, but at that moment the doctor arrived, a tall, authoritative man, and took him by the arm, and turned him round towards South Kensington Station, and told him to follow the road to it. He went off, mumbling about a catastrophe. What is significant is that

Joyce, for all his volubility, could not find an explanation for this incident.

Paying their rent up to the last minute, leaving no tradesmen's bills unsettled, the Joyces moved to a lodging as poor as any he had known since he had left home as a boy. It was a basement flat in a short street of dreary and discoloured houses, mean in size, which lies on the Warwick Road side of Earl's Court Station. Over their roofs, making them more dwarfish, looms the formless concrete height of the stadium; and at the end of the street is the wall of Brompton Cemetery, pierced with openings covered by wire netting, which disclose the sparse tombs among the rank, long grasses on the cemetery's edge, and the distant white crowd of stout Victorian dead round the central avenues. This was not only a melancholy home for Joyce, it was minute, no broader than a henhouse. It might have been chosen by a man who believed himself about to go on a long journey and to need no more than a place to keep his clothes and his baggage till the time came to pack the one inside the other.

William Joyce must have been sure, in the summer of 1939, that there was going to be war, for we were all sure of that. And with half of his mind he knew what part he was going to play in it; but with only half, for again he let his passport expire. He did not apply for its renewal until 24 August; and that date destroys William Joyce's last claim on our sympathies. For it is one day after Hitler signed his pact with Stalin. Then this man who all his adult life had hated Communists must have known that his leader was an opportunist and not a prophet; that he himself was apostle of a policy and not a religion; that there was nothing in the cause to which he had devoted his life that was equal in worth to the ancient loyalties. Now he should have seen what was on the underside of the banners stamped on the overside with the swastika that hung between the sky and the stadium at Nuremberg. Now he should have recognized that the words he had been saying since 1927 were 'Evil, be thou my good'. But he would not open his eyes or unstop his ears, and he stood fast and chose damnation. It is here his happy marriage helped to contrive his doom. He had made his decision to go over to Germany with the knowledge of his wife. To have gone back on it would have been a confession that he had been unwise when he made it; and he may have feared that such a reversal might have looked like a failure in courage. There are risks the most loving will not take with the beloved.

It is said that William Joyce went to Germany on the eve of the war on an off-chance to offer his services to a surprised propaganda machine. But that some people in England were anticipating his departure for Berlin, and tried to stop it, is proved by the recollection of one who in September 1939 was still a schoolgirl. One summer evening she was walking in the Fulham Road with her uncle, a young man who was a member of the British National Socialist League, when they met William Joyce, who was well known to both of them. He seemed strangely excited, and he told them, laughing extravagantly, that when he had been driving his car on the previous day he had been pulled in by the police for a trifling breach of the traffic regulations. The schoolgirl and her uncle were puzzled by his emotion. The uncle said, 'But this is nothing. All sorts of people get run in for motoring offences.' Joyce answered, waving his hat and clapping it back on his head, 'Do you call this a motoring offence? I would call it a holding offence!' and went on his way. A 'holding offence' is a device often and properly used by the police.

When the police suspect a man of a serious crime but cannot prove him guilty of it, they watch him to see if he commits some minor offence, such as a breach of the traffic regulations. If they are lucky and he acts according to their expectations, then they can serve him with a summons, and until he has faced his trial can exercise a certain amount of control over him. During this time they can prevent him from leaving the country. Late in August 1939, in a street near Queen Anne's Gate, William Joyce met an acquaintance who had long ago been his neighbour in East Dulwich, and they halted and had a chat. When they parted, Joyce's acquaintance noted that he turned into the building beside which they had halted, and realized that this was the Passport Office. Even before that the name of William Joyce must have been posted at every port; and as soon as he fetched and had in his possession a renewed passport the warning signal should have been repeated. But a few days afterwards the police were searching for him all over the country; the old lady in Sussex was questioned, and her house was watched. William Joyce had left England by the ordinary Continental route from Victoria, without hindrance. There was either a break-down of routine fantastically fortunate for him or another traitor working with him on the same pattern of treachery.

CHAPTER 6

In Germany autumn is not as it is in England, it is a time not of sleepy mellowness but of bracing magic. The splendid red and gold of the foliage is hard to the eye, the air is like iron; those who sail on the waterways which run all the way from the Wannsee to the Baltic find their lips seared, though they may not feel very cold, by the air which has come down from the Arctic. Into this season, which in its fierce and icy brilliance is one of Germany's particular enchantments, William Joyce was brought by his treachery. One day his little feet twinkled up the area of his basement flat near Earl's Court. His eyes must have been dancing. No matter what his misgivings might have been, the risks of the adventure must have delighted him. It must, indeed, have been intoxicating for him to go through London, where he had never been of any importance, where he was at best a street-corner speaker better known than most, and know that, if he won his gamble, he would return to it as the right hand of its conquerors. There would be then no building he would not have the right to enter, bearing with him the power to abolish its existing function and substitute another. There would be no man or woman of power whom he would not see humiliated, even to the point of imprisonment and death. The first should be last, and the last should be first, and many would be called and few would be chosen, and he would be among those that were chosen. He left the damp and the fog which would soon close in on London, and the obscurity which had closed in on him ever since he was born, and he went out to the perfect autumn of Germany and the promise of power. Very soon he was established in a home in the Kastanien Allee—Chestnut Avenue—in that most delightful suburb of Berlin, Charlottenburg, where there are broad streets and wide-windowed flats and little avenues of villas in flower gardens. On 18 September 1939, exactly fifteen days after the outbreak of war, he joined the German radio as an announcer of the news on the English service, and had very soon become a reader of the news.

His voice was very soon recognized by the doctor and his wife in South Kensington, who had already begun to wonder about their former tenants. When an officer of the National Fire Service had come to examine their attics for combustibility they had found an inexplicable addition to their home. In a cistern loft, accessible only from the flat the Joyces had occupied, a bed had been put up and was there with its bedding. There was plenty of room to put up a bed in the ordinary rooms of the flat; the loft could be entered only by a very small trap-door, and it must have been very difficult to get the bed up through it; there was almost no space to spare round the bed. It must have been put up there during William Joyce's tenancy for somebody who had to be sheltered without the knowledge of the doctor and his wife. Now William Joyce had lost a friendship which he had found it hard to win, and perhaps it occurred to him already that he might have made a bad bargain. He had not been given a warm welcome by his new friends the Nazis. They showed no consciousness of his experience as an agitator, and they underrated his remarkable powers as a broadcaster, and gave him nothing to do but read news bulletins. But he was used to being thought little of by people when he first met them. That the news he was broadcasting was often fatuously untrue, and rendered all German propaganda suspect by its untruth, was probably unknown to him. When he told England that in September or October 1939—long before any bombs had fallen on the British mainland—Dover and Folkestone had been destroyed, he may well have believed it. It is worth while noting that this period of Joyce's service to the Nazis was given an interest in England which it lacked for him. The local details by which Joyce was supposed to show that he had a direct channel of communication with England, such as allusions to stopped town-hall clocks and road repairs, are not in fact found in the records of his broadcasts. They were invented as part of a whispering campaign designed to weaken public confidence, which was carried on by Fascists, some of whom, if not all, belonged to organizations other than Joyce's British National Socialist League. Ignorant of the inaccuracy of his broadcasts, and the use that was being made of them, Joyce may have been bored with his work; but he cannot have felt such a passive emotion about the conditions in which he worked.

He must very soon have looked round the office of the English section of the Rundfunk in panic. It is said that the Duke of Wellington, on seeing some troops for the first time, exclaimed, 'I don't know if these fellows frighten the enemy, but, by God, they frighten me!' So might William Joyce have exclaimed when he first saw the colleagues who had been artlessly assembled by Dr Goebbels' propaganda machine. The most sympathetic among them was an elderly lady called Miss Margaret Frances Bothamley, who before the war had helped to found a body called the Imperial Fascist League and had run it from her flat in the Cromwell Road. She was in a state of extreme confusion. She had brought with her to Germany photographs of the King and Queen and the Princesses, with which she ornamented her flat; and she believed that in her youth she had made a secret marriage with a German music-master named Adolf, whom she appeared to identify with Hitler. During the first months of the war Joyce was forced to recruit a member of Miss Bothamley's organization, who had been spending the summer in Germany: a colonel's daughter who belonged to one of the most famous literary families in England on her father's side and was related to a most exalted peer on her mother's side, but who had, through a series of unhappy accidents, found herself in her late forties lost in less distinguished worlds. She began by being an enthusiastic pro-Nazi, but, being fundamentally not without honesty and decency, turned against the regime, and annoyed Joyce by sitting about in the office and knitting with an air of silent criticism.

There was also Mr Leonard Black, who must have been a disappointing colleague for William Joyce. He was a likeable and talented victim of the toughness of life. Under thirty, he had a long history behind him of inextricably confused idealistic effort and paid political adventure. He had at one time been a member of the B.U.F., but had left it and had later been a paid organizer in the service of the Conservative party, while at the same time—which was odd—carrying on pacifist agitation. Then he went abroad and taught English at various branches of the Berlitz School of Languages, and was so doing in September 1939. It was his story later that the day before war was declared he went down to the station and tried to buy a ticket to England, and, as he had no foreign currency, went home. Few of us do not know the mechanism employed. He had wanted to stay in Germany. He said, 'I ought to go and see about that today. But tomorrow will do just as well. I have a lot to do now. I will go tomorrow.' He did that until one day when somehow it would become possible to put aside all engagements and take the necessary steps; and on that day it happened that those necessary steps could no longer be taken. Then he returned home saying, 'Well, I have done all I could. Nobody could have told that today it would be too late. It is not my fault.' And at the back of his mind a voice must have said with cold cunning, 'Yes, I will be able to tell them that, if things go wrong and I am called to account', while another voice said, 'Look, you Nazis, I have stayed with you.' Most of us—except the people who are in fact intolerable nuisances by reason of their incapacity for compromise—have at some time or other behaved according to this formula. But William Joyce, having just abandoned this formula at the great crisis of his life, was unlikely to feel sympathy with Leonard Black or other recruits of his type.

He owed the presence of Black in his office to the activities of a certain Herr Albrecht, whose business it was to see what Englishmen stranded in Germany would do for their hosts. He sent for Mr Black and a friend of his called Mr Smith and questioned them as to their readiness for cooperation. Mr Black went home and wrote Herr Albrecht a typically ambiguous letter.

> Dear Herr Albrecht [he wrote],
> I write to make it perfectly clear that I have not offered to work for the Gestapo. I would never think of doing that, and I absolutely refuse to sell my country. There is a certain price I will not pay. The most I would do is radio propaganda.

And he ended with a postscript which bears a significance beyond his intention. 'Mr Smith,' he wrote, 'will not even do radio propaganda.' Mr Smith, using that term in its generic sense, did not even do radio propaganda. Only a small proportion of the civilian internees or prisoners of war lost their loyalty; and of those that did, many found themselves too noble to be the instrument of their own ignobility and went back to their camps, where some of them were punished till they died, and all suffered grave torment. They were not many, the men who could split their minds in two and pretend that while they were serving Germany they were making contact with anti-Nazi elements and sabotaging Nazi activity, which was the defence that nearly all of them kept at the back of their minds and produced at their trials. All such men hated William Joyce, who did not split his mind, who desired to make

England Fascist, and, to procure that end, was ready to help Germany to conquer England, and never denied that desire or that readiness, either during the war or after it.

He sat among the hatred of these poor silly creatures, and knew a more humiliating hatred from some others who worked in his office. A certain number of Germans had been drafted into the office, men who had a special knowledge of the English language and English life. As such men had usually acquired their knowledge through having English relatives or having been educated in England, many were anti-Nazi. They despised Joyce as a traitor to his own country, and an enemy to their own country, the true Germany; and they were gentlemen, and cruelly knew he was not a gentleman. But there was another painful element in the office, which must have cut William Joyce far deeper. The Nazis were prone, in all sorts of circumstances, to make a peculiar error. When one of their enemies became their friend, they went on treating him as an enemy. However ready he might be to serve their interests, however much they might need his help, they continued to savage him. The great historic example of this curious trick is their treatment of the Russian soldiers and civilians who, by tens of thousands, gladly surrendered to them as they invaded Russian territory in 1941 and 1942. These people, who might have been their most valuable aids then and for ever after, they packed into cattle trucks and sent off to camps where they were starved and tortured. Later they were fetched out and invited to fight alongside the Germans, but by that time their enthusiasm was not what it had been, and the treatment they received in training and at the front failed to revive it. The Germans acted on the same perverse principle towards the British broadcasters, who were all favourably disposed towards them to start with, and, having burned their boats, had every reason to remain firm in the faith. But at the head of the British section, which they had as if in mockery called the Concordia Bureau, they placed a certain official, who was so hostile as to seem a maniac to many of his baffled subordinates. Throughout the war he maintained this curious attitude to his wretched staff, English and German.

Two Germans were to tell a British court what his rule had been, in evidence that was disinterested and, indeed, unaware of its own portent. When Mr Black was tried at the Old Bailey early in 1946, the prosecution called as a witness one of the German technicians who had recorded his talks. He was an S.S. man, a lank and hollow-cheeked young man, who might have been carved in wood in the thirteenth century, and he spoke a peculiar wooden German which might come to be natural in a man who had been drilled all his youth in tyranny and then marched along a straight road for many years in the direction of defeat. He was called Krumpiegel; surely one might as well be called Rumpelstiltskin. As he gave evidence, there stood beside him the interpreter who was then one of the chief glories of the Old Bailey, that slender and distinguished old gentleman of Spanish-Jewish descent, Mr Salzedo. He was very courteous to the defeated barbarian but plainly savoured a certain satisfaction as, in his silvery voice, he translated the comic expressions used by barbarity. 'Did Black look happy when he was at the Concordia Bureau?' asked the defending counsel. Mr Salzedo translated: 'He says that he does not consider happy [*glücklich*] an

appropriate word to use in connexion with Black's personality, but for the greater part of the war he could fairly be
described as contented [*zufrieden*].' The defending counsel continued: 'But did Black seem to be contented in his
relations with the head of the Bureau?' Krumpiegel looked
more wooden than ever; he folded his arms behind him,
said some words, and looked blank as an ill-treated child
that has told the truth about its tormentors and does not
believe that it will not be punished for it, whatever the
grown-ups say. Mr Salzedo translated: 'He says the chief's
relations with his employees were never a source of grat-
ification.' There came later to give evidence for Mr Black
one of the anti-Nazi Germans who had worked in the
Concordia Bureau, a sad being wearing an air of desola-
tion more usually presented by places than by persons, a
human Golgotha. A question made allusion to this same
chief. The anti-Nazi paused before answering. In accom-
plished, springless, exhausted, pedantic English, he said,
'He was . . . the prototype . . . of the Nazis.' The Concordia
Bureau had been battered by huge irrational waves, tides
obeying the moon of Hell. Joyce must have been devoured
by rage to find himself this man's subordinate. But there
he had to sit, raged at by his superior, with his idiot compatriots around him. There was one last irony in his situation of which, fortunately, he was unaware. Among the
English who had come to Germany to broadcast for the
Nazis, some were Communist agents. The party thought
it wise to have ears and eyes here also. One at least of these
denounced several of the genuine British Fascists to the
German authorities as spies. But in the first years of the
war no doubt these poor wretches refused to worry about

what were obviously only temporary conditions. When there were gathered in as Nazi harvest first Norway, then Denmark, then the Low Countries, then France, there was nothing on earth to prevent the fall of England: and all the poor misfits in the Concordia Bureau must have had their heads stuffed with infantilist dreams. In dreams a fast car, long as a bus, would be sent down to Dulwich to pick up the family and bring them to Joyce's office: which would have been in Buckingham Palace, or in the War Office, or Downing Street . . .

It would, in fact, have been in none of these places. Inexorably the law that to him that hath it shall be given would have come into operation again; there would certainly have come forward as Quislings after the first few days of the German occupation this popular historian and that expert in foreign affairs, this Civil Servant and that leading Communist, and these would have been given precedence over William Joyce, who would have found himself fulfilling just the same subordinate role in the new dispensation as in the old. But that he would not have suspected. He must have imagined himself saying to his father and mother, smiling, 'Well, this is my room. Do you like it? And the next one is mine, too, that's where my three secretaries work.' He would have talked his young brothers and his sister into taking good jobs, and would have found admiring Angus MacNab a post that would keep him close to him. In the evening his wife would have worn fine new dresses, like the wives of Göring and Goebbels, in a home he had no doubt long since chosen as he passed it in his little car, on the way back from a meeting. Joyce's unbeloved *aide*, Mr Black, had friends at Brighton, and, in his daydreams, would have extended his protection to them, for he was generous. They were afterwards to put up bail for him at the London police-court.

Miss Bothamley, no doubt, would have explained the beneficent intentions of the invaders to Queen Elizabeth and the Princesses: and the colonel's daughter, who was a kindly creature, would have looked after the interests of her former husbands. It must have been a sickening blow to the inhabitants of the Concordia Bureau when weeks and months passed, and the Nazis still did not invade Britain. Then came the air-raids, and the apotheosis of William Joyce. He was a revolutionary, which is to say that he hated order and loved it. For the revolutionary wants to overthrow the order which exists because he believes that he can substitute for it another which might be superior. This may be an absence of order which, by a mystical logic, he has proved more orderly than the presence of order. Or it may be an order which, if he be the suicidal type, he subconsciously knows will be inefficient and will thus restore nothingness to a universe so obstinately created, so stuffed with things. But whatever the revolutionary dreams of in the sense of reconstruction, his will is directed towards the destruction of a system which cannot be destroyed. It has come into existence as a result of the interaction of innumerable forces, some invested in man, some diffused through earth and air and fire and water. Not in the short space of even the most massive revolution will the nature of man or of earth and air and fire and water be substantially modified. So when they set to work on a new system it is inevitably very like the old. In revolution there is first destruction of what has been created, followed by its re-creation, on less favourable terms, owing to shock and waste. The appetite for death that is in us all is immensely gratified and that is all.

The French Revolution has given pleasure to all subsequent generations, because it was an outstanding event which afterwards proved never to have happened. A number of revolutionaries overturned the monarchy of France, because of its tyranny and its financial and economic inefficiency, in order that they might substitute a republic which should give its people liberty, make them equal, and join them in fraternity. When the din settled, France was ruled by a self-crowned emperor who wielded power more absolute than any French king had ever been given by the priests who crowned him; and the society which reconstituted itself after his fall conferred on its people increases of liberty and equality and fraternity no greater than were won by other nations untouched by revolution. The Russian Revolution, which is plainly going to be a source of still greater satisfaction, achieved a more perfect balance; for, with an enormously greater expenditure of blood than France ever saw, it slowly reconstituted the Tsardom it destroyed, identical in spirit, allowing for the passage of time, and reinforced in matter. (There is something good in this. The scientific genius of Peter the Great even rises again from his tomb for the delectation of Sir Charles Snow.) William Joyce was among those who set their hands to the Nazi Revolution, which, with an infinitely greater expenditure of blood than either France or Russia had seen, was to tear down Europe, which was then two pence coloured, in order that it should be built up again, penny plain.

Now that the R.A.F. was let loose on Germany the Berlin night above Joyce's head was sprayed with such gold and silver and precious stones as he had seen when he stood with his young wife at the windows of his flat near the Crystal Palace, watching the firework displays. An American correspondent who broadcast from Berlin up to the time of Pearl Harbor has described how one night he could not leave the Rundfunk building because of the bombs and took shelter in the cellar in the company of Joyce and his wife, and how Joyce snarled out in his queer voice a stream of amusing and inventive curses on the raiders. With gusto he sneered at the English over the radio, telling them how their planes were wasting their bombs on the sham cities, *Doppelgänger* Berlins and Hamburgs and Essens laid out on fields with lights, where mock fires were started to make believe they had hit their targets, and rolling on his tongue the 'gross registered tons' of the English shipping which were being sunk by Nazi submarines.

Very early on in this new air war a bomb fell on Michael Joyce's house in Allison Grove. Nothing remained of it except a hole in the ground beside the remains of a neighbour's basement. At the time of his son's trial long grasses and lilacs and syringas, grown wild-branched for lack of pruning, gave the place a certain elegiac beauty. The family lost all their possessions except the trunkful of old papers and a few pieces of furniture, and they went to live at a rest centre until they were found another house. To strangers they seemed arrogant and unmoved by the shame of being kin to Joyce, who by now had been identified by many people, particularly in this district, as the news reader on the German service known all over England as

'Lord Haw-Haw'. But when a worker in the centre came to Mr and Mrs Joyce and told them that she was a friend of the doctor and his wife who had been Joyce's landlords in South Kensington, and that she herself had met Joyce, the old man and his wife broke down. William had always been the difficult one of the family, they said, but they had never thought he would be led away into doing anything so terrible as this, for he had always been a good boy at heart. It was perhaps his trouble, they pleaded, that he was too brilliant. They were ultimately found a house, a character- less little modern villa in an uninteresting part of Dulwich, which must have been too small to hold a family of such numbers and such strong individualities. It is not easy to understand why Michael Francis Joyce, who was by then over seventy, and his wife, who was growing very frail, did not go to the country under the evacuation scheme. But there was no real reason why Lear should have wandered on the stormy heath instead of taking shelter from the storm. Men sometimes feel that if a certain hammer falls it is their part to act as anvil. Michael Francis Joyce lived among the amazement of the news and the bombs until he died five months later, on 19 February 1941.

It is not known whether Joyce heard of the destruction of his family's home and the death of his father at the time of these events; but it is not impossible that he did, however loyally his relatives kept their obligation not to communicate with him, for the Joyces had connexions and friends in both Eire and the United States. Certainly he showed signs of stress, notably in his relations with his wife. That he and his wife loved each other deeply cannot be doubted, but as the war went on his manner towards her struck others as unkind, and their marriage was interrupted by a divorce, which was however followed by a remarriage. His position in the Rundfunk would have been by itself enough to drive a man of his temperament to distraction. He was learning that traitors are in the same unhappy state as prostitutes: their paymasters think they have a right to employ them, but hate and despise them for being so employed. Moreover, his work itself was growing more degraded in kind. From the beginning he had been engaged in the unhandsome business of recruiting announcers and speakers in the camps of British civilian internees; but a gloss could be put on its unhandsomeness. Some of the internees were British only from a legal standpoint, such as people who had been brought up in Germany since childhood or who were the children of mixed marriages; and of these a number were sincerely glad to have an opportunity to perform any service asked of them by what they considered as their fatherland. But as the war went on, William Joyce was obliged to do more and more of his recruiting among prisoners of war, first drawn from the mercantile marine, then from the regular services, the Army, the Navy, and the Air Force. In only a very few cases could Joyce have the slightest reason to suppose that the men he was approaching would have any ideological bias towards Fascism. What he was doing was to seek out men who as prisoners of war were undergoing an extreme physical and mental ordeal, and to bribe them by promises of freedom and food and drink and the society of women into sacrificing their honour: which was no empty phrase in this connexion. When they went to the microphone with William Joyce, they broke their oath of allegiance to the head of their state and cut themselves off from their comrades for reasons that were apparent and contemptible, and they committed, in little, such an act of cruelty to their kin as Joyce had committed to his, on his own grand scale. They transferred their loyalty to the people who were dropping bombs on their parents and wives and children. It was an ugly business, and it grew uglier in the handling.

At first few prisoners yielded to temptation. The British authorities had foreseen the situation and had made provision for it. In theory, all soldiers, sailors, and airmen were warned before they left England that the Germans would ask them to broadcast, pointing out that they could thus reassure their families regarding their safety, and they were ordered to refuse in all circumstances. But even though this theory often broke down, the British officers who were in charge of prisoner-of-war camps under the German staff constantly warned all ranks of the attempts that would be made to seduce them, and kept an eye on those who seemed likely to succumb to seduction.

Moreover, certain men, mostly non-commissioned officers, were given training before they went abroad which prepared them for the ordeal of fooling the Germans and serving as British agents. Few of these Pimpernels came into action at once; so the Germans could count on sometimes getting an odd prisoner who, dazed by shock or by natural imbecility, consented to be interviewed before the microphone regarding the circumstances of his capture. The Germans did not take serious steps to improve this position till 1942, and the big drive they made did not show its results until 1943 and 1944. There were never many traitors, but there were some, and this was inevitable, because the number of prisoners of war was so large that it was bound to include a few representatives of the Fascist minority in Great Britain, and rather more than a few rogues and madmen. Moreover, some sane men were losing their balance under the pressure of the conditions peculiar to the life of a prisoner of war, the worst of which is his uncertainty concerning the duration of his imprisonment.

The most interesting example of the sincere Fascist traitor was a pilot officer in the R.A.F., a man of forty, who joined the S.S. and wrote broadcasting scripts for Joyce. He uttered a revealing remark when a British court-martial sentenced him to ten years' imprisonment for an extreme act of treason which might well have cost him his life. He said indignantly to his lawyer, 'This just shows how rotten this democratic country is. The Germans would have had the honesty to shoot me.' The Nazis made curiously little use of this honest and lettered fanatic or any of his kind. They seemed more at ease with the rogues and the madmen and the sane men off their balance, whom they took great trouble to procure. They established holiday camps, at which the conditions were comfortable and even, to the eyes of many privates and ratings, luxurious; and the German welfare officers in the ordinary prisoner-of-war camp approached men whom they had marked down as likely prospects and told them that, as they had of late been working specially hard or seemed to be in poor health, it had been decided they should go for a month to one of these special camps. It would very often be true that these men were overworked and ill, and therefore the invitation seemed to them a welcome sign of humanity in their captors, and when their own officers told them not to accept it, the advice seemed a sign of their inhumanity. Most of the men thus tempted kept their heads, but some did not. These were exposed during their sojourn in the holiday camp to gentle propaganda, and at the end of the month were returned to the normal discomfort of their original camp. After they had had a few days on which to brood on the change, Joyce or one of his agents paid them a visit and suggested that a permanent return to comfort might be arranged if only they would read some scripts before the microphone. It would be explained that these broadcasts would be extremely pro-British and would simply aim at the affirmation of German goodwill towards Great Britain, and this was often true, for this was the early radio policy of Dr Goebbels.

All these proceedings were quite uneconomic. The money was laid out to little purpose, and there we have come on an early instalment in a serial story which has become progressively more dismal. Expenditure on weapons may at least bear indirect fruit in the form of advances in scientific knowledge, but every year more and more money is spent by the great powers in maintaining an army of traitors and spies, many of whom serve imperfectly the purpose for which they were hired, and can make no contribution to any higher purpose. How this operated in the Second World War on the German side can be judged from the tale of Mr Walter Putney, the son of a Barking widow, a junior engineer on H.M.S. *Vandyke*, who was captured at Narvik. He was an eccentric creature with some real but superficial ability, but he cannot have done much for the Nazi cause. Joyce wrote broadcasts for him to speak over the air, but these were not among his best. Joyce was a passionate and sincere anti-Semite; every time he spoke of those whom he called, in a drawled, sneering dissyllable, 'The Jeeoos', his acquired accent cracked and fell away and his strong native Irish had its way. Not surprisingly, the anti-Semitic material he wrote was his weakest.

As well as broadcasting some very unseductive material of this sort and dealing with it in leaflet form, Putney consented to go to the famous British prison camp of Colditz to spy on the occupants, but there he broke down and gave way to a Dostoyevskyan weakness for confessional collapses and told all to a Senior British Officer. This was a typical adventure. Prison camps are not funny places, but poor Putney nearly made them so. The complications he created, the trouble he caused both British and Germans can be judged by what he did after the peace. He was a very lucky man, soon finding his way out of the nightmare that all the traitors knew at that time: they were treated like unloved children whose parents are doing a moonlight flitting, stuffed into a van, and told to hold their noise or else. The S.S. sent him with a mixed bag of traitors down to Italy, and there they were moved about from town to town until he and a Dutch broadcaster stole a motor-cycle and rode towards the German front lines, where they managed to be captured by Italian partisans, who, thinking they were ordinary prisoners of war, handed them over to the American Army. It repatriated Putney to London, where he gave an immensely long statement to Scotland Yard, which had only had incomplete reports on him and decided it could not be bothered about him, as it had so much more important business on its hands. His life and liberty were handed back to him on a platter. Putney then proceeded to get himself into trouble all over again. He fell in love with a young typist; and his emotion had the curious effect of making him write a complete account of what he had done in Germany. This was many thousands of words long and was almost the same, sentence by sentence, as the statement he had given to the police weeks before. He put this in an envelope and gave it to the typist, telling her she was to send this to a solicitor if he should be arrested, a possibility he had not been able to dismiss. He then had the extreme imprudence to fall out of love with her before recovering the envelope. She opened it and read its contents, which were a complete surprise to her. From motives not of greed but of anger, she told him she would take the letter to the police if he did not give her a sum of money far too large for him to raise. This threat need not have meant anything to Putney, as it was a replica of the statement he had already made to the police. However, it inspired him to go to the nearest police station and, in a dramatic monologue delivered with great force and brilliance, appealed to the law to protect him against this attempt at blackmail.

The dazed constabulary appealed for guidance to Scotland Yard, which had, by an unhappy coincidence, just received much fuller reports of what Putney had been doing in Germany; and he was arrested, and charged with high treason, because he was suspected of betrayal of the secrets of his fellow-prisoners at Colditz, though on that charge he was acquitted. But on the other charges, which related to his broadcasting and the preparation of leaflets for the S.S., he was found guilty and sentenced to death.

He was returned to Wandsworth Jail, where William Joyce was awaiting execution, and was put in another condemned cell, but hardly noticed it, being rapt in a new interest. The police like no crime less than blackmail, which is indeed an icy sin, far farther from love than murder. As soon as they had Putney's case well under way they prosecuted the typist for demanding money from him with threats, and immediately Putney became inflamed with a desire to give evidence in her favour. The girl, however, pleaded guilty and was bound over. The prosecution was quite clear that she had probably not meant to collect the money and was simply expressing jealousy. It is probable that disappointment over this anti-climax clouded Putney's relief when, after his appeal had been rejected, he was reprieved.

It is to be noted, as characteristic of the problems of security and espionage and treachery, that this eccentric had occupied the time and energies of a large number of Germans. It had taken a welfare officer, someone referred to as a *Gruppenführer* (who might be any one of a number of persons of minor authority), and William Joyce to recruit him. Once he was incorporated into the system, he was dealt with by a small army of men who had university degrees or service rank—Dr Springberg, Dr Kurt Eggers, Dr Menzel, Dr Zeigfeld, Dr Adams, Dr Hafferkorn, Dr Wansche, Dr Hempel. They lavished interviews and correspondence and telephone calls on him, and at least two S.S. agents (including one bearing the delightful name of Herr Wockenfuss—'Mr Distaff-foot') seem to have followed him about for long periods. It is hard to avoid suspecting that the organization of British treachery had become a racket, and that a number of Germans were exploiting it to find themselves easy and remunerative jobs at a safe distance from the front; and that their success was not paid for in efficiency. In spite of all this wealth of personnel German security was not good. Labour in Berlin being short, four British prisoners of war were once sent to do the cleaning in a villa used by the German Foreign Office; and all four spent some time sitting on the floor and reading the contents of the waste-paper baskets, being highly trained Intelligence agents. What was more, they had the means of communicating their discoveries direct to England.

All this must have disgusted William Joyce, with his pride in his own competence. It is possible that he may have been revolted morally. He does not seem to have been a sneak; and he cannot have liked a stratagem employed to overcome the reluctance of prisoners to turn traitor, which is worth noting because, like the uneconomic nature of treachery from the employer's point of view, it has endured until the present day. There were British subjects who said that they might have considered broadcasting but were restrained by the fear of what would happen to them if the British won the war; and they were told that this was no real obstacle. 'You can always say that you thought you would have a better chance to escape once you were out of the camp and that you meant to send messages home over the air in code, or put sugar into the petrol tanks of vehicles, and were in general carrying on a private war against the Nazis. Nobody will be able to say you did not.'

The traitors accepted this idea, which is proof that excessive egotism is an ingredient in treachery. It never occurred to any of them that if this advice was proffered to him it would be proffered to a number of other people. Hence, at court martial after court martial, soldiers and airmen turned up with defences which were often word for word the same, a coincidence which could not but be remarked. This ingenuous practice has been carried on from the time when traitors were Nazi to the new age of the Communist traitor and still persists. The Germans must have known that the prescription is unlikely to work, but they did not care. They were cruelly indifferent when they overcame Mr Putney's timidity by helping him to find an alibi in advance. He carried on a prolix and animated correspondence with his family in London, suggesting in veiled terms, by mis-spellings and snatches of verse, that he was incorporating in his broadcasts information to the Royal Air Force about the weather over Germany and the probability of German raids over England. If he ended with 'Good night', there would be no raid, but if he said, 'Good, good night', the German bombers would be over. His family, highly respectable and well-meaning people, gave them to a Red Cross official, who forwarded them to the proper quarters. Putney stuck to his story to the very end, and only when he was under cross-examination in the Old Bailey did he realize that the British authorities knew that his broadcasts were not live but recorded, and that the recordings were not always used the same day that they were made. It follows that his warnings must always have been valueless, and he must have known this; and the Germans must have known that the British authorities would know that Putney knew this. The lot of traitors is very hard indeed.

The Concordia Bureau was getting shabbier and shabbier; it was providing broadcasters for what was known as the

New British Broadcasting Station, which pretended to its listeners that it was operating on British soil. One broadcaster,
with a duplicity which would never have been suspected in
one who privately was full of idealist pretensions, frequently
tried to convince British listeners, by assuming a Cockney
accent and the sort of wheeze affected by impersonators of
Dickens characters in order to breathe, 'You'll probably 'ear
us tomorrer night at the same hour, but it's getting 'ard, the
Police are always on our 'eels nowadays.' Another speaker
called himself Father Donovan, but was obviously not a
priest, since his chorus-boy falsetto would have led to his
rejection by the broadest-minded seminary, and in fact was a
seaman in his late twenties. It is unfortunately not open to us
British to laugh at this ridiculous enterprise, since the Allies
engaged in similar follies. There was 'clean' broadcasting,
which told the truth, and 'dirty' broadcasting, which took
the proposition that the end justifies the means and bolted
with it. The bolting went so far that there were sent over the
air in the Allies' name such nasty fantasies as broadcasts
purporting to come from microphones secretly installed
in the bedroom of an enemy leader who was raping a girl.
These broadcasts are objectionable not only in principle, but
are also injurious to the morale of the people whose officials
sent them out. Either the people detect the fraud and learn
to distrust their own government, or they do not detect the
fraud and come to believe such falsities as the existence of
sympathetic and constructive resistance movements in the
country they are fighting, where in fact these do not exist
at all, or exist in quite a different form.

William Joyce was contending with imposture and
idiot companionship. A fair sample was an eccentric and

passionate Salvation Army officer who, knowing either less or more about Eva Braun than we do, believed that the personal purity of Hitler was about to redeem the sinful world. He also lost some of his better comrades. He had not liked the colonel's daughter on his staff. But after sitting about the Concordia Bureau for years knitting in a sullen manner, she made her departure in a way which must have compelled his respect. She gathered her tattered integrity about her, sold all she could lay her hands on to pay back to the Germans every mark they had ever paid her, and was swept off into a concentration camp, from which she was to emerge, at the end of the war, into twelve months of prison and such subsequent exclusion from the society of her kind, such bleakness and hopelessness, that one may count her as having paid her bill and more. She was the victim of denunciation by a fellow-traitor. The organization was ravaged by conflicting forces.

The troubles of the Concordia Bureau were not merely internal. Though a small staff of British was working for the German Foreign Office, the Concordia Bureau was a part of Goebbels' Propaganda Office, which was the hated rival of the German Foreign Office. The primary cause of the rivalry between these Ministries was the fact that the Propaganda Office was a Nazi creation and the German Foreign Office was full of Junker staff whose roots had not been torn up during the Weimar Republic because they had been so deeply planted in the soil of Germany under the Hohenzollerns. The rivalry had deteriorated, as all else in German life, and had become something very like a struggle between two gangs to get the bigger share of loot in a 'protected' area. Perhaps because of simple departmental jealousy, and perhaps because of the large number of jobs connected with the Concordia Bureau, the Foreign Office took more and more interest in the Bureau as the war went on. The office must have looked like any manifestation of the civil service, but actually insane cantrips were taking place. The official later to be called 'The prototype of the Nazis' was now a prey to ungovernable rages, and once had it in his mind to send the inoffensive Mr Black to a concentration camp, for what reason no one could ever discover. The people who intervened and saved his life were members of the German Foreign Office staff belonging to the group concerned in the attempt on Hitler's life in 1944. They were apparently anxious to take control of the Concordia Bureau out of Goebbels' hands. There were political cross-currents here which resulted in the arrival of a visitor to Berlin whose presence must have seemed to William Joyce a gross personal slight.

CHAPTER 7

John Amery, who at the time of his trial had lived thirty-three years and had been in trouble for most of them, was the son of a gifted Englishman who had rendered liberal service to his country, and his wife, who was loved by many for her kindness.

John Amery was not insane, he was not evil, but his character was like an automobile that will not hold the road. As a child, he would be taken by his parents to a hotel at some holiday resort and would be discovered in a corner of the gardens or in the lounge, after dinner, amusing the guests with some mimicry or musical fooling. But the entertaining monologue would become a dribble of nonsense, the dance would go on too long, and there would break in a hint of frenzy. The child would turn from a pet to a pest, and sooner or later there would be trouble of an odd, unpredictable kind arising out of behaviour which was not cruel or cowardly but slapped the normal process in the face. What is one to do with a boy of fifteen who from school issues prospectuses for a film-producing company and collects money from investors, not with the intention of embezzling it but inevitably with that effect? What is one to do with him when he is so pitifully delicate that it is not possible to subject him to the discipline of work? One can but say hopefully that he will not always be fifteen. This is, however, not necessarily true. There are some who are always fifteen. When he came to Berlin he was as the years went about thirty. He had been convicted seventy-four times for automobile offences, which included some quite unforeseen embroideries on the commonplace process of travelling from one point to another with the aid of an internal combustion engine. Marriage he had complicated as effectively as transport, credit to him was what orchestral tone is to a conductor, and his business enterprises were unimaginable. He once stranded an entire motion-picture outfit in Africa in circumstances which struck even the motion-picture industry as extraordinary. When he was twenty-four his loyal but exhausted family let him become bankrupt. He failed for five thousand pounds and his assets were nil. He went abroad on a generous allowance, so generous that it meant some sacrifice for his parents.

This was in 1936; when the Spanish Civil War offered a theatre for both left-wing and right-wing gallants, John Amery was a not-unsuccessful volunteer on Franco's side. He had a fairly continuous career serving as a gun-runner and as liaison officer with the French Cagoulards. When the war broke out he remained on the Continent, still travelling between Paris and Madrid, and it is believed that the traffic which he carried on then took a reverse direction and that his Cagoulard friends now received arms and money from certain Spanish elements to aid them in their opposition to the war against Hitler. It is useless conceiving of Amery as either a mercenary trafficker or a dogmatic Fascist.

At the fall of France he fled to the south of France; but the Vichy Government, which was trying to preserve its credit with the French people by dissociating itself from the frankly pro-German Cagoulards, and which was irritated on its prudish side by his revelry, treated him as an unwelcome guest. Its distaste for him increased, and at the end of 1941 it put him in prison for eighteen days and released him on condition he lived in the mountainous district round Grenoble. He was at the time, so those that saw him say, very addled, very bored with the provincial life to which he was thus restricted, and in need of money. It is not surprising, therefore, that he offered his services to the Italians, who never answered his letter, and then to the Finns—then engaged in their anti-Soviet war—who declined them.

But the local German armistice chief, Graf Ceschi, took him under his protection. Amery said that this association was not of his seeking, that the overtures came from the Graf, and in view of what happened this is not incredible. In the autumn of 1942, a German officer took him and a French woman who was perhaps his wife to Berlin. There they were received by a Dr Hesse, who belonged neither to the German Foreign Office nor to the Propaganda Office, but to Hitler's personal staff. Thereafter, for a period of several months, John Amery was the most petted and best advertised English propagandist that had ever been put on the German radio. Immense trouble was taken to draw the world's attention to his broadcasts, which were repeated several times in an evening on one particular night in the week. He was given luxurious hotel accommodation, with a heavy expense account. He was sent all over Europe to address internment camps and give interviews to the local Press, and he was photographed and filmed as if he were a Hollywood star.

In many ways Amery must have got Joyce on the raw. Amery was an Englishman, and the conflict between England and Ireland had never quite resolved itself in Joyce's mind. He adored the English, he had fought for them as a boy—or had at least performed some services which he thought of as fighting for them—and he genuinely believed that as a Fascist he was labouring to confer benefits on England. All the same, it was to England that he had come as a boy and had been sniggered at as a queer little bog-trotter with a brogue. It was England which had been ungrateful to his father and refused to compensate him for the loss of his property in Ireland. It was in England that he had been denied the power and position which he felt to be his right by virtue of his intellect. Ancient hatreds, however much they may be adulterated, often revert under stress to their first purity. When William Joyce cursed the raiders who were bombing Berlin, he cursed them as an Irishman cursing the English. Now here an Englishman had come, late in the day, and was put ahead of those who had been drudging in exile for years.

Moreover Amery was a gentleman. He had been born on the imperial side of the River Thames, heir to every advantage which William Joyce had craved, and he had thrown all of them away. He had a right to despise Amery morally; for though he liked a glass of whisky as much as the next man, he kept himself hard as nails for his work and paid his debts. As for his intellectual superiority to Amery, that must have stung him. He had a limited but avid mind and he had tried to put some thought into his broadcasts whenever the Germans gave him the chance. Words flowed from Amery's mouth in the conventional groupings of English culture, but he had no intelligence, only a vacancy round which there rolled a snowball of Fascist chatter picked up from Doriot and Deat. Yet here he was installed in a suite at the Kaiserhof while Joyce had only a flat in the suburbs, with an unlimited expense account which meant opulence compared to Joyce's unimpressive salary; and here was the German radio cupping its hands round its mouth and shouting to the whole world that it must listen to Amery's broadcasts, though they could have no propaganda value whatsoever.

That Amery was an excellent broadcaster, that the radio, which is one of the greatest liars in the world, transformed him into a pure and eager boy, burning with sincere indignation at the moral evils of Bolshevism, was beside the point. He was known to every newspaper reader in England as the problem child of distinguished parents, who had made countless appearances in the police courts, and the sole result of putting him on the air would be to make English listeners feel sympathy with his family and a reiterated conviction that the Germans were terrible cads.

Worse still as propaganda was Amery's project, known at first as the Legion of St George. This was a body to be drawn from British prisoners of war who were to fight alongside the Germans against the Russians to save Europe from Bolshevism and the idea of it made the former director of Mosley's propaganda squirm in his seat. None knew better than he did what chance there was of raising such a legion. He knew that only a sprinkling would join and that these would be mad or bad. He knew also that a recruiting campaign conducted by John Amery, accompanied by a female companion whose appearance would be interpreted by the ordinary soldier as a call to the joys of peace rather than to the tasks of war, would make English treachery a laughing-stock; and traitors have their pride like other people. He must have perceived that the Germans were in some ways very stupid, and perhaps he doubted whether they were going to gain the victory which was necessary if he were ever to realize his ambitions or even save his life.

Yet German propaganda was perhaps never less stupid than in the exploitation of John Amery. For propaganda has many uses beyond persuasion. What it sometimes aimed at in this case can be deduced from the character of Amery's gospel, considered in conjunction with the date. Though Amery's speeches held a few drops of anti-Semitic poison, his real preoccupation was hatred of Russia and Communism. He made it a condition that the Legion of St George should be regarded as an exclusively anti-Bolshevist force, and should be used only on the Russian front; his conception of the war was as a struggle between holy Nazism and corrupt Communism, contrived by the Jews, and he wanted not peace but another war in which the West should sink its differences in order to attack the Soviet Union.

Now in the autumn of 1942 the Germans were beginning to feel nervous. It had appeared from the end of August that the situation in North Africa might not end as they wished, for Rommel's great offensive had been halted, and that because of his lack of aircraft. The Allies' air attacks on Germany were becoming more and more formidable. The Japanese were not doing so well as had been hoped. A group of Germans in and around the Foreign Office were not certain that Germany was beaten; but then again they were not certain that it was going to win. So they formed the idea that it had better sacrifice some of its ambitions and get rid of some of its liabilities. If they could stop war with Russia, so rashly initiated in 1941, Germany would have its energies free to fight Great Britain and the United States. But if it was to start peace negotiations with Russia these must be kept secret, for two reasons. One was that if Great Britain and the United States heard of them they might use argument and force to dissuade the Soviet Union from the proposed desertion; and the other that, even if this persuasion by Great Britain and the United States failed, they would surely cut off the stream of supplies which they were sending out to the Soviet Union. But these shipments would be continued to the last moment before the breach and would be shared with Germany when it again joined forces with the Soviet Union. It might throw dust in the eyes of Great Britain and the United States if, just at the time when these secret negotiations were opened, the Germans started a new anti-Bolshevik campaign. They made their first overtures to Moscow, and John Amery was fetched out of his retreat in Savoy in October 1942 and broadcast during the first part of 1943 and began his recruiting tour of the camps. Nobody else could have drawn such widespread attention to an anti-Bolshevik campaign. If William Joyce had made these broadcasts and gone on that recruiting tour, not a soul would have taken the slightest notice. It was the unique and fatal distinction of John Amery to be the one person out of the earth's population who could serve the German purpose; and the Nazis did not mind looking fools so long as they could create the impression that they were still actively anti-Bolshevik.

It is to be remarked that from the middle of 1943 the fortunes of John Amery suffered a marked decline. The negotiations between Germany and Russia had broken down. It appears that only a small group had ever participated in them, and possibly that group was not influential. He was no longer welcome in Berlin; and when he lost most of his personal belongings in one of the famous raids which, on every night between 22 and 26 November 1943, assailed Berlin, he was awarded a decoration for exceptional bravery and packed off to Paris. From there he was sometimes sent to the occupied countries, such as Norway, Belgium, Czechoslovakia, and Yugoslavia, out of sheer nastiness; to prove that the British were degenerate, that a leading British statesman could have a son who betrayed his country and hiccoughed as he did it. Soon they stopped letting him do even that, and in September 1944, with savage and indecent irony, they sent him down next to act as confidant to Mussolini, now at liberty and a poor figure of fun after his undignified rescue from Allied hands. 'Enter Tilburnia, stark mad in white satin, and her confidant, stark mad in white linen.' What is the sin against the Holy Ghost? It is perhaps to deal with people as if they were things.

In Germany, William Joyce sat and waited for the end. He moved about; most often he was in Berlin, but sometimes he was in Eupen and at Luxembourg, at the end he was in Hamburg; but always there was over him the same sky, the *mitteleuropäische* sky, which is clearer than the English sky and is not loaded with dreary fogs, but has its own nocuments, which are madness and defeat. He was involved for the last year or so in the aftermath of the unfortunate harvest of Amery's brain, the Legion of St George, known as the British Free Corps. After Amery had been ejected from Berlin, having served the Nazi purpose, the Legion had been handed over to the S.S. and its name had been changed to the British Free Corps, and its recruits either were drawn from Joyce's broadcasters or broadcast for him afterwards. This must have been sheer torture to Joyce. Some of them were pathetic. One, Kenneth Edward, had been taken by the Germans off a torpedoed ship when he was fourteen, kept in a prison camp for two and a half years, and then recruited by John Amery, whom he believed to be Foreign Minister of Great Britain who had somehow been ejected from his country and was being kindly assisted by the Germans to regain his rights. Another had given a false age when he volunteered for the British Army in 1941 and was just seventeen when he was captured in Italy, and he believed that the British Free Corps was six divisions strong. Some had another significance, such as Herbert George.

He had not the excuse of youth as these two had; but on the other hand it could be said that he had been in such trouble all his life that he had had no time to grow up. He was of medium height and had the look of a Disney dwarf, but not a happy one, for too often the Thames-side police courts had claimed him. Once a chicken had been stolen; then a gas-meter slot had been opened and emptied; once someone had missed a shirt and a scarf. It was too much. He had attempted to commit suicide, and when he had served the mild punishment inflicted on him for that offence he enlisted in the Army, but they would not have him, he was discharged as unfit. This was, however, only the beginning of a military career which was to be unique. He had always been interested in politics, and when the Spanish Civil War broke out, he volunteered to serve in the International Brigade and actually fought in Spain. He soon deserted, and the incident was purged of the sordid by the candour with which, having crossed the Pyrenees and reached the Channel on foot, he sought the London offices of the International Brigade and reported as a deserter. Hurt at his reception, he went to sea and continued as a sailor after the war broke out. In 1940 he was taken off an oiler torpedoed in Norwegian waters, and was in one prison camp and another until 1944, when he received a letter from his mother telling him that his wife had had a baby. After thinking this over for some time he decided that it could not be his baby and was deeply distressed, and when two merchant seamen came to enrol recruits for the British Free Corps, he enlisted, just as a sad little dog, finding himself far from home in streets where they throw things, with rain falling and the dusk thickening, will follow any passer-by.

Herbert George is not a negligible figure. There are so many of him.

Some of the British Free Corps had a great deal more excuse than the poor little man. Six of them, known as the Big Six, had natural endowment and education enough to realize what they were doing. One, the son of a Lithuanian merchant settled in England, had been at an English public school. It was surprising that he should have been in the British Free Corps, for he was a Jew on his father's side. He may not have known this, for he had been brought up out of contact with his father's family, though the Germans must have known it if any intelligent officer examined his papers. He joined because he wanted to find himself a niche in the international society which he thought would be erected after the inevitable defeat of the Allies. Another of the Big Six, Francis —, a qualified pharmacist, had been a member of the British Union of Fascists from 1934 to 1938, but this need not have been a determining factor which made him a traitor. He had been a sergeant in the R.A.M.C., and being captured at Dunkirk, was sent to work in a prisoner-of-war hospital in Poland.

There he was caught breaking a rule and was told that he was to be sent to the worst camp in Poland, which was famous for its abominations. Rumour had it that there the starved prisoners fell on the bodies of their comrades that dropped dead and tore out their liver, their kidneys, and the soft part of the thigh, and ate them. An American prisoner who was found in the camp when it was liberated has testified that this happened, though not many people could bring themselves to do it because the bodies were so lousy. To avoid being sent to this camp, Francis wrote to the authorities stating that he wanted to join the Waffen S.S. and fight the Russians. That he was moved by the desire to

save himself from this hell cannot be regarded as an absolute excuse, for thousands of men, finding themselves in
the same position, chose to suffer the pains of hell rather
than buy themselves off by complicity with their torturers.
But few of us would care to judge him. It is to be noted
that Francis was perhaps the nearest to a Mosleyite traitor
that the Second World War provided. The other adherents
of the B.U.F. who appeared among them had lapsed from
membership some time before the outbreak of war, and
their cases prove nothing except that silly young men were
apt to join the B.U.F. in some circumstances and in others
were apt to become traitors. Neither here nor in any other
theatre of war was there proof that the B.U.F. had issued
instructions to any member of the Armed Forces.

The most obvious trace of ideological action in the
camp was furnished by two priggish little negativists
named Denis John and Eric Reginald. Denis John was the
son of a stoutish middle-aged man, with watchet-blue eyes
and a quiet way with him, who owned two baker's shops in
North London, notably bright and clean for the grey streets
of those parts; a German, the son of a German immigrant,
who had had the sorrow of feeling it his duty to fight the
Germans in the First World War. His son could not feel
it his duty to fight them in the Second World War, for his
parents' marriage had broken up when he was seven years
old and he had been brought up by a German grandmother
and had been at school in Germany, and there had been
a lot of trouble. He did not want to be a baker, for one
thing; and he was a Lohengrin or Siegfried, with clear-cut
features and waves of blond hair like golden wire, and he
drew to himself the attentions of some young people with

more money than he had, who, according to his family's friends, did him no good. When the time drew near when he should register for military service he felt a natural reluctance to fight against Germany, which, strangely enough, he, a German's grandson, knew and loved better than his father, who was a German's son. If he had gone to the proper authorities they would have explained to him the means by which people in his position could appeal for exemption from military service as conscientious objectors.

But some of his new friends persuaded him to go to the offices of a pacifist organization and ask for assistance in evading military service, and it was arranged that he should take advantage of a scheme which exported registered conscientious objectors to do farm work in various districts, including the Channel Islands. It is not clear how Denis John was brought under this scheme; he never claimed to have become a conscientious objector, and cannot have been registered as one, for he had never even been called up. He was under age. But Denis John was sent off on a travel warrant issued by the Ministry of Labour to Jersey, which, neither in this war nor the last, would ever have seemed the safest of refuges, but was particularly unsafe on the day of his departure, which was on 17 May 1940, seven days after the Germans had invaded the Low Countries. It is not at all surprising that by August Denis John was working for the Todt organization, the Nazi sappers; and the office which had sent him to Jersey must have been unusually silly if it felt astonishment at that, though it had no guile in planning these events. There was not even the sense of a treasonable agreement behind these imbecile proceedings. The Germans were not prepared to accept these unhappy children, and Denis John and a number of others were dragged about Europe, from camp to camp, for five years, exposed to every sort of degrading influence, till he and Eric Reginald landed in the British Free Corps.

They joined it apparently only because the recruiting leaflets had caused an uproar in the English prisoner-of-war camp where they happened to be and they wished to show how superior they were to the common herd. The men who now were their comrades were a pitiful crew. They had all left their camps after being warned by their senior officers that they were taking a step which would cut them off from the society of their own kind, and passed into a state of degradation which made it inevitable that society would carry out its threat, not from nursed intention but as a result of the natural recoil from something that stinks. The Germans had, of course, far too much sense to keep on with the Legion because they thought they could raise enough men to form a fighting unit for use on the Russian front or anywhere else. They wanted them for quite another purpose.

They put these men in villas in various pleasant parts of Germany, and dressed them in German uniforms with flashes with the letters B.F.C. and the Union Jack to show that the wearers were British soldiers, and let them go rotten with idleness and indiscipline and debauchery. They did a little drill and learned German and, as one of them said, 'otherwise did nothing except lay around, and go into the town, where we drank and associated with women'. There were never many of them. It appears that of the hundreds of thousands of prisoners of war in Germany only thirty odd volunteered for the corps. But even so small a number, split into groups and sent into the German towns, drunken and with prostitutes on their arms, did something to raise national morale in 1944 and 1945 and persuade the Germans that it was all true, what they had been told, and that they could not possibly be conquered by those degenerate people, the British. It is worth while looking at these drab and debauched people because this type of traitor was not to pass away, but was to reappear on the other side of the world in another phase of time.

With what horrified embarrassment this crowd of scallywags was regarded by William Joyce, who had been so proud of his association with the Worcestershire Regiment, who carried himself like a midget sergeant-major, can be judged from the effect they had on a young man called Thomas Haller Cooper, who was very different from William Joyce except for his detestation of what comes 'all along o' dirtiness, all along o' mess, all along of doing things rather more or less'. Cooper's father, a photographer in south-western London, had been a soldier in the Army of Occupation after the First World War and had brought home a German bride. When he was nineteen his mother took him back to Germany, as a woman taking her child to present him at the temple, herself returning to London. The year was 1939. A short time after war broke out he joined the Adolf Hitler Division of the Waffen S.S., and served in Poland, and then in Russia, where he was wounded. When he was convalescent he was recalled to do traitor's work, visiting the English prisoner-of-war camps and talking with the prisoners and giving them corrupting literature, and finally was made an N.C.O. in charge of the British Free Corps and practically became Camp Commandant.

At first he enjoyed the work, and many of the members of the British Free Corps liked him. There was probably a real geniality, an honest tenderness, between them. Cooper had come from the Eastern Front, the others had come from years of hunger and confinement; they found themselves clean and well-fed, and could exchange tales of woe in what was their native language and his father's tongue in a good villa that was more than comfortable, that was cosy, among the woods, the sweet aromatic German woods. He was a good-looking young man, tall and slender and dark, with that neatness which amounts to a form of piety, a cry to Heaven for approval. He had the look of the more thoughtful of many young Germans who became Nazis: the look of the white-collar man who cannot climb up because he has no special talent to make his own ladder and society will not let him use its existing ladders, which are reserved for other people.

Spiessbürger is the German word for it. He was loaded with frustrated ambition. He had been a clerk in London, and had tried hard to get out of the groove. He had a great love of the East, and though he had not a very good record at school, had worked hard at learning Japanese and Chinese, and as he reached his later teens he tried to find employment in branches of the government service which might take him to the Far East, but was rejected because his mother was a German. For the same reason he had been rejected as a candidate for the English and Colonial police force. The conflict in the boy's mind regarding the nationalities of his parents must have been painful, the more so because his mother was a woman of distinctive character. Her home was distinguished from all other dingy houses in the road by the wealth of flowering bulbs, jonquil and narcissus, crocus and grape hyacinth, which crammed the bow windows. This interesting parentage was, however, denied him by the Germans. He was presented to the British Free Corps as the son of Mr Duff and Lady Diana Cooper, a remarkable fatuity, since the sophisticated members must have realized that the only child of the most publicized character of our time was not yet of military age.

Cooper travelled all over Germany with his charges. (It is one of the curious features of the Nazi regime that it made the German passion for travelling into a guiding principle of its administration. Prisoners of war, whether loyal or traitors, were moved round and round and round the country long before the time when they had to be hustled out of the way of invading Allies. It is as if in England we had moved the prisoners we held in the Isle of Man to the West Highlands, to Wales, to the Isle of Wight, and so on.) Always the billets were good, comfortable villas with gardens, set among the woods and heaths. The custody of these louts was not the enterprise Thomas Haller Cooper had foreseen when he was detailed to it, and he found he could keep himself sane by withdrawing into his favourite and unusual studies. In his room, instead of the usual portrait of Adolf Hitler, there hung a fine Japanese print. He had a solemn and sentimental love-affair with a respectable young girl called Gisela, to whom he expounded Oriental philosophy in immensely long letters. He was really only a boy. In company he would murmur, as if in absence of mind, such phrases as *Om mani padme hum*, and on being overheard and questioned as to what they meant, would start, give a translation, and explain that such phrases were always running through his mind, since he was, as a matter of fact, a Buddhist. At the same time he showed himself to be a Western reading schoolboy under the skin, by boasting quite untruthfully that he had come to Germany because, in an East End street fight, he had killed a Jew. Unfortunately his confidant was a British agent.

But no amount of sitting about in the sun among the pines and mooning over Oriental grammar and writing to Gisela could reconcile him to the degradation of his charges. He tried to apply a mild form of S.S. discipline to them, and they mocked at him and staged a mutiny. He behaved with courage. But when D-day came and went, and the gales blew and did not blow away the Allies, and the Atlantic Wall was as if it had never been, then he was frightened. He said, 'I have been a bloody fool', and announced his intention of working thereafter 'for the other side'. But again it was to a British agent that he said those words. Thereafter this strong and proud young man had to cringe and smirk and flatter in the hope of survival. He was obliged by orders of his superiors to visit prisoners of war and thrust kindnesses on the prisoners under the sceptical eyes of noncommissioned officers, terrible beings, worst when they were little creatures burned up by Indian suns till there was left in them not a scrap of blandness. These looked straight at him and without speaking said things about rats leaving sinking ships. But these missions were easier than his duties at base with the British Free Corps, who daily grew more drunken, more desperate, more maudlin in the arms of their whores. Often they openly cursed him and disobeyed his orders, and sometimes he let it pass, because he did not dare to do anything else, but at the same time he was prodded in the back by his superiors, who did not know yet whether they were beaten. If they were beaten, they meant to pull off their jack-boots and run; but it was hard to find this out for certain, and in any case they had obeyed orders for so long that they had forgotten how to take the initiative. Everybody's brain was boiling.

Sometimes authority thought that, yes, it would pull off its jack-boots, and left Cooper to do what he would with the British Free Corps. Then he and his louts sat in a kind of vacuum. The authority would change its mind and would buzz about Cooper's ears again, and ask what he was thinking about to let discipline run down, and he would disentangle the louts from their disconsolate female friends and insist they do a little drill. On the night of 13 February 1945 authority finally lost its head. The British bombed Dresden, as a result of an order which has since been studied exhaustively but which remains mysterious; and they slaughtered thousands of refugees and turned to rubble one of the fairest cities bequeathed to our time by people possessed by virtues which we lack. Authority then announced to the unit that it was to be sent to Russia. At this news the British Free Corps took to its bed as one man. Authority then turned on it, and alleged that in some way the Corps was responsible for the bombardment, and clapped them all in prison. Some of them had been there already. The baker's son, Denis John, and his companion, Eric Reginald, had only joined the British Free Corps to flout the prejudices of their fellow prisoners of war, and once they were in the Corps organized a revolt among the confirmed rebels, such as the poor little Herbert George, he who had always been in trouble—chickens, the gas-meter, the International Brigade. For that they were sent to a *Straflager*, a punishment camp, and learned what it could be like to be entirely protected, either by the police or by the recognized authorities of a prisoner-of-war camp. After seven weeks they had petitioned the German authorities to let them go back to the British Free Corps on any terms, and were allowed to do so. The Corps, on hearing it was faced as a whole with a *Straflager*, revolted. Authority was overcome by panic, and pretended to take seriously the complaints against Cooper. He walked off with a straight back, to be captured by the British, sentenced to death, and reprieved.

William Joyce now sat in his office, conducting his business with a quiet sacramental order. He had become wholly reconciled to his wife. D-day had been a crushing blow to him. All through his life he had been anxious, with the special anxiety of a very small man, not to make a fool of himself, and the first consequence of such wariness is to dread making prophecies that prove untrue. In his broadcasts he had mocked again and again at the idea of an Allied invasion of the Continent; and they had often been followed by songs, abominable and amusing lyrics coldly and lightly sung, which jeered at the Englishmen who were to attempt invasion and would lie dead under the Atlantic Wall. But now the Atlantic Wall had been broken. He had made a fool of himself.

Also he realized that, if the Atlantic Wall was broken, it did not matter how much effort it had taken to break it; henceforth it was insubstantial as a dream. Henceforth, it was not to be Germans who were to kill Englishmen. There were perhaps to be more Germans killed by Englishmen than Englishmen killed by Germans, perhaps Germany itself was to be killed, perhaps William Joyce himself was to be killed, certainly William Joyce was to be killed. That possibility had always been clear in his mind. In his preface to his book, *Twilight Over England*, published in Holland in 1942, he had written:

> When, however, the writer is a daily perpetrator of High Treason, his introductory remarks may command from the English public that kind of awful veneration with which £5,000 confessions are perused in the Sunday newspapers, quite frequently after the narrator has taken his last leap in the dark.

He must also have been conscious of what had happened to him. He had proved that there are no half-measures in treachery. If a man does not love his country enough to concede its right to self-government, he will end by not loving it at all, by hating it. Again and again Joyce had spoken with icy approval of the murder wrought by Germans on his fellow-countrymen. He had not felt this unnatural emotion was important, for it was temporary; he would go back to England as a bearer of benefits, and would be reconciled to his own people. But now he had to wonder whether they would forgive him; not forego punishment, that he knew could not be, but forgive him.

As a revolutionary he must have known a sort of peace as catastrophe flowed towards him from the east and the west during the first months of 1945. There had been much doing and the fruit of it was to be nothingness; there had been a fullness of life, there was to be an emptiness of death. To this end he had worked since youth, and he would have been disappointed by victory. But that he himself should die must have brought him the torment which the prospect of death brings to us all. That is the weakness of the revolutionary idea: human beings only want to play with the idea of death, they do not want to die.

Waiting for the end, William Joyce sat in his office and distracted himself by doing his work extremely well. His last broadcasts were, in form, ably and carefully written political essays, much superior to anything he had put over the air up to that time. In substance they were self-exculpatory. They warned England that she was being ruined by her participation in the war, and, destitute, would have to face a new and insatiable imperialist Russia; and rebuked her for having fought Germany instead of aiding her to fight against the Bolshevization of the world. This was nonsense. The week before Germany had brought England into the field against her by invading Poland she had signed a pact with Russia, and she remained in close friendship with her for the best part of two years; and no intelligent Englishman had wanted his country to go to war with Germany, because none was unaware that, if the price of defeat would be the reign of the Gestapo in England, the price of victory would be the disruption of Europe, the destruction of its political and economic and intellectual harmony, which is the highest level man has yet attained. It was the horrible and unique achievement of Hitler to force the West to fight the most terrible of wars without the sustenance of faith in victory. So the tired man, night after night, stood in the Hamburg studio of the Rundfunk and warned his fellow countrymen of a danger which they had always anticipated and which now no longer could be avoided. There came a night when he spoke as if he were either very tired, or drunk, or perhaps both. Then, on 30 April 1945, he made a broadcast in which, speaking slowly and with dignity and obstinacy, he admitted defeat. It ended with the sentence: 'Britain's victories are barren; they leave her poor, they leave her people hungry; they leave her bereft of the markets and the wealth that she possessed six years ago. But, above all, they leave her with an immensely greater problem than she had then. We are nearing the end of one phase in Europe's history, but the next will be no happier. It will be grimmer, harder, and perhaps bloodier. And now I ask you earnestly, can Britain survive? I am profoundly convinced that without German help she cannot.' Saying these words, he plainly thought himself a statesman, but he had said nothing that could not be answered with a phrase from an old comedy, *'Tu l'as voulu, George Dandin!'* This was the last time that the insatiable hunger of his voice was to travel over the air. English soldiers came into his office a day later and found it not disordered but empty.

CHAPTER 8

Each traitor took a different path to the end. Some hid themselves and were never found, and one of these was of some importance. But most of them found their way to the court martial or the Old Bailey, and there revealed more of themselves than might have been expected. For most of them were destitute, and had to take advantage of the Poor Prisoners' Defence Act, and a lawyer chosen under this Act has not the usual amount of control over his client. He cannot tell him to go to the devil and find another lawyer, should he disregard advice; hence many traitors made the mistake of giving evidence on their own behalf and gave away much that might otherwise have been concealed.

Most of them walked to the Allied lines and presented themselves as escaped prisoners of war. The men who followed this course enjoyed a false sense of security which lasted for some time. Their stories were naturally accepted, and those of them who had acquired a good working knowledge of the German language during their captivity were useful as interpreters to the advancing British and

American troops. Such men continued in this magical state of immunity for a matter of weeks or months. Till VE-day and for a long time after, the Army had many other things to do than to chase unimportant traitors; and during this period of disorganization the men were sheltered by the rule of the British Free Corps and the British section of the Rundfunk that all traitors except the most important should work under assumed names. This did no more, and the Germans must have known it would do no more, than give them a short respite before arrest.

Little Mr Black reported at the British Embassy in Brussels, making no secret of having worked at the Concordia Bureau but claiming that he had merely sought cover for doing kindnesses to victims of Nazi persecution. One of the more hopeless members of the British Free Corps carried on him to the end the photographs of thirteen German prostitutes, as well as mementoes of a steadier attachment. John Amery was captured by the partisans in Italy; and when he was questioned by a British Military Intelligence officer he asked for a typewriter and proceeded to type a statement some thousands of words long, which was brilliantly composed, put the noose around his neck, and gave the history of two different people. One of these was a wise young man of lofty principles who sought to reconcile England and Germany in order that together they might fight the rising tide of Communism, and to that end travelled about Europe, a weary Titan urging common sense on statesmen who for some reason would not heed the voice of sanity; the other was a crazy harlequin enmeshed in unfortunate adventure. 'After a few days in Paris, and travelling under the names of Mr and Mrs Browne, I arrived in Berlin early in October 1942', he wrote. For a time this inveterately companionate 'I', who was always travelling under the names of Mr and Mrs Somebody, was to be alone. 'On 7–8 April', he wrote, 'my beloved friend and political revolutionary, Jeannine Barde, died'. The poor creature's death was said not to be natural. By some accounts she killed herself, life being rendered unendurable by the sour flavour of treachery, the air-raids, the humiliations of dependence on the openly contemptuous Nazis, who knew that these two had no alternative employers. By other accounts she died because of a blow received at a wild party. The Germans' feeling for etiquette was outraged by Amery's failure to attend her funeral, though as like as not it was through unbridled grief that he absented himself. But to the wandering wit sorrow is no prison.

> In the end of September [he wrote] I returned to Paris. Once more much political talk, and on 4 October I remarried at the German Consulate. Politically, the situation remained almost unchanged.

And at the end of the statement comes Harlequin's supreme antic. This man awaiting a capital charge writes:

> Moreover, the colonel commanding the Piazzi di Milano, who brought me from Saronno to Milan, undertook at the time to have returned my property that was seized by the partisans when they arrested me. Of this nothing has so far been seen. It consists of one suitcase (important documents and personal

effects), one overcoat, one fur coat, and two silver foxes, a 20-litre petrol tin, full, one Lancia Aprilia motor car No. 78410 MICDI.

A statement well worth reading was contributed by Herbert George, the Disney dwarf. He described how he met a German girl called Hilda Henschel, and after speaking to her found she was pro-English.

> I told her I wanted to escape, and she said she would help me. I told her I had studied the theory of piloting a plane and eventually she told me she could find out where I could get hold of a plane, which she did. The plane was in an aerodrome about thirty kilometres away from Hildesheim. On the night we had a nasty raid and the airfield was damaged so I could not carry out my plans.

He returned to England, and at his Thames-side home rejoined his wife in perfect domestic bliss, although he had taken steps to divorce her when he was in the prisoner-of-war camp; and, determined to pick up all the threads, he became the life and soul of the local Communist party. The poor little man had to leave this happy and busy life for two years' hard labour.

It would have seemed a pity to have bothered about this odd little soul, but such segregation was in his own interests. It was certainly a great relief to the licensed trade of his Thames-side town. On Saturday nights Herbert George would come into a bar and after a drink or two would be filled with a desire to entertain the company and would therefore relate his adventures, first in the International Brigade and then in the British Free Corps. This never worked out well. His imprisonment must also have been a relief to the officers of the local Communist party, who were doubtless serious-minded men. This odd creature, and all the other odd creatures, then went into a world abhorrent to contemplate: a world of cold cells, of dirt, of mind-slaying monotony. Not that it would have mattered so much to this most resilient of prisoners.

William Joyce left his broadcasting office and went out, in the company of his wife, to seek a safety which, by then, he knew could not be found. First he slipped into his pocket a passport made out in the false name of Wilhelm Hansen. It is significant that the imaginary Hansen was described as a teacher. Joyce liked teaching, he was proud of his gifts as a teacher. It was dated 3 November 1944, but the date may have been as false as the name. It is unlikely he would have given in and taken this precaution till the last possible moment. Then it would be easy, for all over Germany people were sitting in government offices forging papers to deny their curious Christs at the third cock-crow. Joyce's wife had a separate passport. It had occurred to them that anything might happen: the worst might happen; they might have to part. So they started on their journey, and, like all the traitors who then closed the door behind them on the misery and futility which had grown thicker and thicker round them for the previous five years, they stepped out into the spring. But not for the Joyces any season of respite, for they could not, like their underlings, go into the British or American lines and tell a lying story and be given work, and be at ease for a little and hope for the best. Joyce, who at that time had only a vague suspicion that there was any doubt about his British nationality, knew that there was no hope for him at all if he fell into Allied hands; he had issued too definite a challenge.

So the Joyces went out into the forest, the beautiful German forest towards the Danish frontier. They made their headquarters in a country inn in a pleasant village on the wood's edge, and by day they impersonated a German couple on holiday. They were now united in their earlier love, though they must have been troubled by self-reproach. Each must have said, 'No, it was not your fault we came from England, it was mine.' At all times they were horribly uncomfortable. The Allied troops were everywhere, and they were under a real necessity to hide. They ate at irregular intervals on what they could get, and William Joyce had always been exacting, in his sergeant-major way, about his food. They both grew very thin, and could not keep themselves clean or neat. Joyce developed a skin disease affecting the scalp.

On 28 May 1945 they had been on the run for some weeks. That evening he was walking among the trees near Flensburg, when he came on two English officers, Captain Lickorish and Lieutenant Perry. Had he gone on his way they might not have noticed him, for he was by then a miserable figure, and they were busy in searching for kindling wood. But he halted and watched them, and in the end he had to speak to them. He had been reared by his father to regard the British Army as the symbol of the power and glory of earth; he had hoped to be a British officer himself; he had boasted as a boy that he had served under the orders of British officers. Also they were men of his own people, from whom he had been exiled for five years and more. He called to them in French, 'Here are a few more pieces.' Nothing was more certain to catch their attention. They stared at this strange little figure who was talking French to them in the depth of the German forest. He said in English, 'There are a few more pieces here.' He was lost. At once his voice betrayed him.

The two officers conferred together, and Lieutenant Perry said, 'You wouldn't happen to be William Joyce, would you?' Joyce put his hand in his pocket, meaning to draw out his forged passport, and the Lieutenant, nervous as every member of an invading force must be, thought that he was feeling for a revolver, and drew his own and shot him in the leg. Joyce fell to the ground, groaning, 'My name is Fritz Hansen.' But so little store had he set on his sole means left him for escaping detection that he had not troubled to memorize his own false name. His passport was made out to Wilhelm, not Friederich, Hansen; and he was still carrying his real military passport, made out in the name of William Joyce.

One of the officers went away and made contact with authority; and eventually Joyce was taken to the military hospital at Lüneburg. Mrs Joyce had been arrested and taken to a prison camp, spent and dishevelled, saying in her habitual manner, which was jaunty and mechanically cynical, that she and her husband had expected this for a long time and that there was no use making a fuss about it. They were not to see each other again until after he had been sentenced to death. The news that Joyce was coming to the hospital arrived before him, and his stretcher was carried from the ambulance through a crowd of soldiers

who were chiyiking and crying out, 'This is Jairmany calling.' This must have been the first intimation to him that
he was considered by the British public as a comic character, and there could be no more perplexing anti-climax. On
31 May an Intelligence officer came and sat by his bed and
interrogated him. To that officer he dictated this statement:

I take this opportunity of making a preliminary
statement concerning the motives which led me to
come to Germany and to broadcast to Britain over
the German radio service. I was actuated not by
the desire for personal gain, material or otherwise,
but solely by political conviction. I was brought up
as an extreme Conservative with strong Imperial-
istic ideas, but very early in my career, namely, in
1923, became attracted to Fascism and subsequently
to National Socialism. Between the years of 1923
and 1939 I pursued vigorous political activities in
England, at times as a Conservative but mainly as
a Fascist or National Socialist. In the period immediately before this war began I was profoundly
discontented with the policies pursued by British
Governments, first, because I felt they would lead to
the eventual disruption of the British Empire, and
secondly because I thought the existing economic
system entirely inadequate to the needs of the times.
I was very greatly impressed by constructive work
which Hitler had done for Germany and was of the
opinion that throughout Europe as also in Britain
there must come a reform on the lines of National
Socialist doctrine, although I did not suppose that

every aspect of National Socialism as advocated in Germany would be accepted by the British people.

One of my dominant beliefs was that a war between Britain and Germany would be a tragedy, the effects of which Britain and the British Empire would not survive, and I considered that a grossly disproportionate influence was exerted on British policy by the Jews, who had their reasons for hating National Socialist Germany. When, in August 1939, the final crisis emerged, I felt that the question of Danzig offered no just cause for a world war. As by reason of my opinions I was not conscientiously disposed to fight for Britain against Germany, I decided to leave the country since I did not wish to play the part of a conscientious objector, and since I supposed that in Germany I should have the opportunity to express and propagate views the expression of which would be forbidden in Britain during time of war. Realizing, however, that at this critical juncture I had declined to serve Britain, I drew the logical conclusion that I should have no moral right to return to that country of my own free will and that it would be best to apply for German citizenship and make my permanent home in Germany. Nevertheless, it remained my undeviating purpose to attempt as best I could to bring about a reconciliation or at least an understanding between the two countries. After Russia and the United States had entered the war such an agreement appeared to me no less desirable than before for, although it seemed probable that with these powerful allies

Britain would succeed in defeating Germany, I considered that the price which would ultimately have to be paid for this help would be far higher than the price involved in a settlement with Germany.

This belief was strengthened from month to month as the power of Russia grew, and during the later stages of the war I became certain that Britain, even though capable of gaining a military triumph over the Germans, would in that event be confronted with a situation far more dangerous and complicated than that which existed in August 1939; and thus until the very last moment I clung to my hope of an Anglo-German understanding, although I could see that the prospects thereof were small. I know that I have been denounced as a traitor and I resent the accusation as I conceive myself to have been guilty of no underhand or deceitful act against Britain, although I am also able to understand the resentment that my broadcasts have in many quarters aroused. Whatever opinion may be formed at the present time with regard to my conduct, I submit that the final judgement cannot be properly passed until it is seen whether Britain can win the peace. Finally, I should like to stress the fact that in coming to Germany and in working for the German radio system my wife was powerfully influenced by me. She protests to the contrary, but I am sure that, if I had not taken this step, she would not have taken it either. This statement has been read over to me and it is true.

(Signed) William Joyce

This was a remarkable statement to be dictated by a man who had been brought into hospital three days before, not only wounded but suffering from malnutrition and exposure. Of course it was nonsense. It would certainly have been in Great Britain's interest to form an alliance with a strong and sane Germany, in order that the political and economic balance of Europe should be maintained. But it was to nobody's interest to be yoked with Hitler, who was for internal and external unrest. Had Great Britain submitted to Nazi Germany few characteristically British people would have survived to have the benefit of Nazi leaders in a war against the Soviet Union. They would have died in British versions of Buchenwald and Belsen. That was why, whether Britain could win the peace or not, she had to fight the Second World War. Nevertheless the statement was remarkable as the effort of a beaten and exhausted man.

Sixteen days later Joyce was flown to England. One of the soldiers in the plane asked him for his autograph as they were crossing the Channel and he wrote him a scrawl—'this is the most historic moment in my life, God bless dear old England', which reeked of that illiterate quality never dispelled by his university education. He was taken to Brixton Prison and there did well. He had, after all, escaped from the alien forest, he was no longer forced to take part in an alien tragedy out of which he might well have contracted. He had food to eat, a roof over his head, and the English about him, the unexcitable, matter-of-fact, controlled English whom he admired. There were no Nazi officials here and no concentration camp. He had always liked the police and got on well with them, and his passion for discipline was so great that he may have found a sort of pleasure in conforming to prison routine. Into this cold grey snugness came his family, most often his beloved and loving young brother Quentin. From them, it is true, he must have learned that though his parents had not actually been killed by the forces whose cause he had espoused they had been tormented by them in their last hours. It is possible that he may have heard of his father's death not long after it happened, for Michael Joyce had died before America had come into the war, and the Joyces had relatives in the United States, but it must have been now that he heard for the first time of the death of his mother. That tiny and spirited being had been persuaded to go into the country after her widowhood, but had returned to London to be with her sons and daughter, and when she was stricken with a painful disease she was taken to St Mary's Hospital, Paddington, where she lay dying during the summer of 1944, while the V-1s broke over the town.

But to distract Joyce he now was faced with an intellectual exercise more complex and more unusual than any he had engaged in when he was free to study as he liked. When he had entered prison he believed he had no defence to the charge of high treason which had been brought against him. But his solicitors drew his attention to the passage in his statement in which he had alluded to his belief that his father had been a naturalized American citizen, and had forfeited his naturalization by failing 'to re-register'. If his father had been a naturalized American citizen when he was born, they told him, then he himself was an American citizen by birth, and nothing which had happened afterwards could affect that. Did he ever believe that safety lay in that resolution of his doubts regarding his status? It may be so. But it is said that, in conversation with a prison official, he described the defence which was to be put up for him and added, with a faint smile, 'It will be amusing to see if they get away with it.' Perhaps the gentle cynicism was honest enough. He had lived by his ambition. That part of his ambition which lived on his lips and in the forefront of his mind had been utterly frustrated. He was not going to be king. In all the world there was not one man, not the most pitiful blind beggar nor the most eroded leper, of whom it could be more certainly said that he would never, till the end of time, exercise the smallest grain of power. The other ambition, which lived in his heart and in the secret governing chamber of his mind, was utterly fulfilled. The revolution had succeeded. He had seen Hamburg, and knew that more than a city had been destroyed; he had a nice historic sense and perhaps he recognized that a civilization had been murdered. Into his cell, each morning, came something like the white light which comes at dawn into a house where a corpse lies awaiting burial. If the dead were loved, then those who wake and see such light feel grief; if they were hated, their enemies wake to emptiness and bereavement, because the hunt is over. If the corpse were both loved and hated, then those that still live feel aching conflict; and if the corpse died not a natural death but had been helped on its way, then their own consciences tell them that they should pay for their guilt with their own lives. The successful revolutionary feels all these things about life, which he has killed in part. Hence his own death is truly a release from pain, and Joyce went serene to his trial, which was not like most earthly trials, but was the pattern of such trials as must happen in the hereafter. For we shall be judged at the end unjustly, according to the relation of our activities to a context of which we, being human and confined to a small part of time and space, know almost nothing. It is said that in few murder cases has it been wise for the accused person to give evidence on his own behalf, but here was a trial where a person under a capital charge could not conceivably give any evidence bearing on his guilt or innocence. He might, indeed, have embarrassed the prosecution to the point of impotence if he had given false evidence that he had not used his passport for the purpose of leaving England for Germany; and he must surely have known enough of the means employed for getting German spies in and out of England to have been able to spin a plausible tale. But he was not a perjurer. He had chosen to play out his drama in the real world. If sentence was to be passed on him, let it be based on the truth. But that condition was all he could contribute to his own trial. He could not speak of his own knowledge concerning his father's naturalization, or his status at birth, or the kind of allegiance he owed to the Crown, or the consequences flowing from possession of a passport. He might have been the poor soul in a theologian's dream waiting to hear if the divine caprice poured wine of grace into his cup and made it saved and unbreakable, or left it empty and damned.

He was found guilty and he was taken to Wormwood Scrubs; a prison standing on the western edge of London next to a school and a hospital on flat and greasy fields where the seagulls gather. It has a peculiar character, for it was built about seventy years ago in the full flush of the late-Victorian enthusiasm for social reform, with the intention of reclaiming prisoners serving their first sentence by providing them with beautiful surroundings. It is a work of great vigour, which recalls at one and the same time Ravenna and Pisa and a giant model of a lodging-house cruet, and it has the merit of presenting extraordinary shapes which the inmates may well find appropriate to their own extraordinary destinies. A prison built as simply as the ordinary hospital or school might well seem heartless to convicts who know that they have lost their liberty by no event as natural as falling sick or growing up, and the oddity of the Scrubs is like a recognition by authority that life became quite strange and different from other people's when a demon entered into them and they said 'Yes' when they should have said 'No'. It was there Joyce waited for the hearing of his appeals, in which he did not believe, and changed to the man we saw at his later trials, who no longer troubled himself about his demon's unfortunate reply, but pondered on an answer he must make to another question.

As it happened, the prison was seized by a spasm of madness and ejected him. The news that Joyce was within its walls spread among the other prisoners, and they raged against his presence. Perhaps they were trying to upset the social verdict of worthlessness passed on them at the same time as their legal conviction; perhaps they were idiotically responding to the call of tradition, for throughout history treason has always been the crime most abhorred by the English, as parricide has been the crime most abhorred by the French. Perhaps it was true of the criminal population, as it was of the rest of us at the end of the war, that the sanest were a little mad and the half-mad quite demented. Whatever their reasons they howled against him with the simplicity of wolves. In his cell he heard the riot, lifted his eyes from the book he was reading and forced them back again, but finally laid the book aside and said hesitantly to the prison official who was sitting with him: 'Those people are not calling out against me, are they?' He received an evasive answer, but was later to learn the truth, for one day as he was taking exercise some prisoners in cells overlooking the yard realized his identity, and, though they knew they would be punished for it, shouted curses at him and threw down on him what missiles they could find through the windows. It is said that some of the craziest convicts formed a plan to make a dash past the warders at a favourable moment, to seize William Joyce and to murder him.

There was little reason for fearing that this plan could have been carried out, but this was not the atmosphere in which a man under sentence of death could be left to await the hearing of his appeal. So Joyce was taken away from Wormwood Scrubs and sent to Wandsworth Jail, a shabby old prison, black as a coal-tip, set among the trodden commons and the discoloured villas, the railway viaducts and the long streets of little houses, which lie 'south the river'. The last days of his life in London were to be spent only a mile or two from the house in Longbeach Road where it had begun. Now his second wife, with whom he had lived only in his aspirant exile north of the Thames, was received into the district which was his real home. A man condemned to death has the right to see whom he chooses, and the authorities brought his wife over from Germany and lodged her in Holloway Prison, sending her over the river to visit him almost every day. They took great delight in each other's company; and on the morning of his hanging she retreated into a frenzy of grief which for long did not abate. It was necessary afterwards to send her back to Germany, for she had automatically become a German subject when her husband became a naturalized German. There it was necessary to put her in a camp from which she was not released for two years, for she was passionately pro-Nazi and could no more be let loose than any other Nazi propagandist; and, indeed, had she been allowed to return to England and her own family, she could not have been left at liberty, for her own sake. These two people had contrived their own ruin with a finality that not their worst enemy could have achieved by unremitting malice. Iago was a gentle child compared to their suicidal selves.

CHAPTER 9

But there remains a mystery about William Joyce and all his kind of Fascist leaders. Why is it so important to them that they should stand on the political platform, hold office, give commands with their own voices, and be personally feared? A man who is not acceptable as a national leader is given by our system the opportunity to exercise as much political power as is necessary for his self-respect and the protection of his rights. He can vote in parliamentary and local elections; and he can serve his country as a private Member of Parliament or a member of a local authority or as a member of a special committee. Why should William Joyce and his kind howl after impossible eminence when in the common run they have no occasion for humiliation? There are other means of establishing exceptional value. If Joyce was not loved by the mass he was loved well by some near to him, and to some was a good lover; to his brother Quentin and to his second wife he was light and warmth. He was also a very good teacher. Happily he transmitted knowledge, and was happy to see it happily received. That surely should have been enough for him: to be a good brother, to be a good husband, to be a good teacher. Many are given less. Yet he hungered for the mere audience, for the wordless cheering, the executive power which, if it be not refined to nothing by restraint, is less than nothing.

Perhaps right was on his side. Perhaps it is not enough to be a good brother, or to be a good husband, or to be a good teacher. For human relationships are always qualified by questioning. A brother, and a wife, and pupils have their own selves to maintain, so they must sometimes defend themselves and keep back their secrets. They will sometimes pass over to the attack and seek out the secrets of the brother, the husband, and the teacher, and often time changes them so that there is no acceptance, only this questioning. It would be better for a man to have a relationship with a person who knew all about him and therefore had no need to question him, who recognized that he was unique and precious and therefore withheld no confidence from him, who could not be changed by time, though by his steadfastness he might change time and make it kind and stable. Those who believe in God enjoy such a relationship. It would be impertinent to speculate about Joyce's relationship with God, about which we know nothing relevant save that he left the Church in which he was born, accepted its comfort before his death, and in the meantime inscribed himself on the Nazi records as a 'believer'. But it can be taken that his mind had been trained over the trellis erected round him by society, and that that trellis was cut in a non-Christian or even anti-Christian pattern. Whether he enjoyed his relationship with God or not, he must often have believed that it did not exist.

Those who have discarded the idea of a super-personal God and still desire an enduring friendship must look for it in those fields of life farthest removed from ordinary personal relationship, because human personality lacks endurance in any form of love. The most obvious of these is politics. There a leader can excite love in followers who know nothing of him save his public appearances. That love is unqualified; for no party can cause its enemies to rejoice by admitting that its leader has any faults, and what parties profess they soon sincerely feel, especially in crowded halls. That love swears itself undying, too; for no party can afford to let itself be overheard contemplating the exchange of its leader for another.

Therefore many men who would have been happy in the practice of religion during the ages of faith have in these modern times a need for participation in politics which is as strong as the need for food, for shelter, for sex. Such persons never speak of the real motives which impel them to their pursuit of politics, but continually refer, in accents of assumed passion, to motives which do indeed preoccupy some politicians, but not them. The chief of these is the desire to end poverty. But William Joyce had never in his life known what it was to be hungry or cold or workless, and he did not belong to the altruistic type which torments itself over the plight of others; and indeed there was probably no callousness in this, for surely if he himself had been destitute he would have been too completely absorbed in his rages and his books to notice it. His was another hunger, another chill, another kind of unemployment. But the only people in the generation before him who attacked the governing class had been poor or altruist, and since their attack had been successful their vocabulary held a twang of victory, and William Joyce and his kind borrowed it.

Therefore they spoke of economics when they were thinking of religion; and thus they became the third wing of a certain triptych. In the third and fourth centuries of this era Europe and North Africa and Nearer Asia were racked by economic problems caused by the impending dissolution of the Western Roman Empire. The study of economics was then barely begun; there was as yet no language in which the people could analyse their insecurity and design their security. But several men of genius and many of talent had been excited by the personality of Christ and excited by the bearings of his gospel on the discoveries made by the ancient philosophers. Hence the science of theology was developed to a stage where intelligent people could grasp the outlines with which it delineated universal experiences, and applied its phraseology to their particular experiences. Therefore those suffering economic distress complained of it in theological terms. They cried out to society that its structure was wrong, in terms which, taken literally, meant that the orthodox Christian faith was mistaken; they rushed from the derelict estates where they starved as peons and sought the desert, where they could eat better on brigandage, and said that they did this because they had had a peculiar revelation concerning the Trinity. The hungry disguised themselves as heretics. Now, in our day, those suffering from religious distress reverse the process, and complain of it in economic terms. Those who desire salvation pretend that they are seeking a plan to feed the hungry. Between the two wings of the triptych shone the rich panel of European civilization, created during a happy interim when, for various reasons, man found it easy to say what he meant.

It is undignified for a human being to be the victim of a historical predicament. It is a confession that one has been worsted, not by a conspiracy of enemies, nor by the hostility of nature, but by one's environment, by the medium in which one's genius, had one possessed such a thing, should have expressed itself. As harsh as it is for an actor to admit that he cannot speak on a stage, for an artist to admit that he cannot put paint on canvas, so the victims of historical predicaments are tempted to pretend that they sacrificed themselves for an eternal principle which their contemporaries had forgotten, instead of owning that one of time's gables was in the way of their window and barred their view of eternity. But William Joyce pretended nothing at his trials. His faint smile said simply, 'I am what I am.' He did not defend the faith which he had held, for he had not doubted it; he did not attack it, for he had believed in it. It is possible that in these last days Fascism had passed out of the field of his close attention, that what absorbed him was the satisfaction which he felt at being, for the first time in his life, taken seriously. It had at last been conceded that what he was and what he did were matters of supreme importance. It was recognized that he had been involved by his birth in a war between the forces in the community which desired to live and those which desired to die, a war between the forces in himself which desired to live and those which desired to die. It was an end to mediocrity.

He said that he had had a fair trial; but he had had two trials. On the floor of the courts where he was put in

the dock there was tested an issue of how far the letter is
divorced from the spirit, an issue which must have come up
again and again since the birth of law. Centuries ago, or in
the part of the world least visited by civilization, it might
be debated whether a man can live all his life among a tribe
and eat its salt and in the hour of its danger sharpen the
spears that its enemies intended for their attack on it, and
go free because he had not undergone the right ceremonies
which would have made him a member of that tribe. But
in the upper air above the courts it was argued whether the
God with whom man can have a perfect relationship is the
dream of disappointed sons imagining a perfect Father who
shall be better than all fathers, or is more real than reality.
This other trial was not concluded, for it began with some
remote birth and will not now end till the last death. It is
this uncertainty which gives life its sickening and exquisite
tension, and under that tension the fragility of William
Joyce was as impressive as his strength. He sat in the dock,
quietly wondering at time as it streamed away from him;
and his silence had the terrible petitioning quality we had
heard in his voice over the air. He had his own satisfaction.
He had wanted glory; now his trial gave him the chance to
wrestle with reality, to argue with the universe, to defend
the revelations which he believed had been made to him;
and that is about as much glory as comes to any man. But
treason took to itself others not so fortunate.

McNally Editions reissues books that are not widely known but have stood the test of time, that remain as singular and engaging as when they were written. Available in the US wherever books are sold or by subscription from mcnallyeditions.com.

1. Han Suyin, *Winter Love*
2. Penelope Mortimer, *Daddy's Gone A-Hunting*
3. David Foster Wallace, *Something to Do with Paying Attention*
4. Kay Dick, *They*
5. Margaret Kennedy, *Troy Chimneys*
6. Roy Heath, *The Murderer*
7. Manuel Puig, *Betrayed by Rita Hayworth*
8. Maxine Clair, *Rattlebone*
9. Akhil Sharma, *An Obedient Father*
10. Gavin Lambert, *The Goodby People*
11. Edmund White, *Nocturnes for the King of Naples*
12. Lion Feuchtwanger, *The Oppermanns*
13. Gary Indiana, *Rent Boy*
14. Alston Anderson, *Lover Man*
15. Michael Clune, *White Out*
16. Martha Dickinson Bianchi, *Emily Dickinson Face to Face*
17. Ursula Parrott, *Ex-Wife*
18. Margaret Kennedy, *The Feast*
19. Henry Bean, *The Nenoquich*
20. Mary Gaitskill, *The Devil's Treasure*
21. Elizabeth Mavor, *A Green Equinox*
22. Dinah Brooke, *Lord Jim at Home*
23. Phyllis Paul, *Twice Lost*
24. John Bowen, *The Girls*
25. Henry Van Dyke, *Ladies of the Rachmaninoff Eyes*
26. Duff Cooper, *Operation Heartbreak*
27. Jane Ellen Harrison, *Reminiscences of a Student's Life*
28. Robert Shaplen, *Free Love*
29. Grégoire Bouillier, *The Mystery Guest*
30. Ann Schlee, *Rhine Journey*
31. Caroline Blackwood, *The Stepdaughter*
32. Wilfrid Sheed, *Office Politics*
33. Djuna Barnes, *I Am Alien to Life*
34. Dorothy Parker, *Constant Reader*
35. E. B. White, *New York Sketches*
36. Rebecca West, *Radio Treason*
37. John Broderick, *The Pilgrimage*